AQUAPONICS & MICROGREENS

The Complete and Easiest Guide 2021

Table of Contents

Introduction

Inside of this bundle you'll learn about the Aquaponics gardening and about the Microgreens.

An aquaponics garden allows a gardener to steer clear of chemical fertilizers using fish to supply nutrients for plants. The plants develop into some soil-free surroundings, and also the roots wash out the water to fish. Collectively, the plants and fish operate together so that the water could be recycled forever.

In the course of recent years, enthusiasm for nearby, crisp, and natural nourishment has been on the ascent. There has been a restoration of the little homestead and a reestablishment of thankfulness for new vegetables. The recovery of the rancher's showcase, the commencement of the CSA model (Community Supported Agriculture), and the general development towards perfect, entire nourishments has been phenomenal and is proceeding to develop.

Individuals are rediscovering the significance of crisp, privately developed nourishment. This development has indicated that it isn't only for the well-to-do, for those keen on cultivating, yet for the entire of the populace and people in the future.

These publication is designed as a starting point for producing a backyard aquaponics and microgreens system. It summarizes how aquaponics works along with the essence of this symbiosis between these components. Additionally, it comes with a concise breakdown of the several sorts of aquaponics methods, also trouble-shoots some frequent issues faced by house growers.

It's a long-term target, however, imagine how wonderful that meal of fish, and fries, and salad will probably be when grown on your aquaponics system.

Chapter 1
The History of Aquaponics and How Aquaponics Works?

Twenty-first century Aquaponics is the tradition of increasing vegetables and fish together in a symbiotic recirculating system. It's a union of hydroponics and aquaculture by which fish produce compounds which simplifies the costly chemical fertilizers applied in hydroponics. In turn, the plants oxygenate the water to allow it to be convenient for your fish, substituting costly filters and aeration equipment employed in aquaculture.

History

Even the Aquaponics movement might appear to be always a rigorously 21stcentury movement, and its prevalence within the western environment is undoubtedly restricted by our period. But, Aquaponics Has historical origins from the Americas and in Asia. Also, we observe that Aquaponics is part of nature.

Back in Nature

Aquaponics is somewhat a rediscovery of good sense principles exemplified in natural ecosystems. We find aquatic plants cleanup water to fish and we all view those plants growing since they're fertilized by fish waste. Whenever the water process has been a moving one, like a flowing flow we view that a version for its circulating water from Aquaponics.

In the Americas

A number of those Fundamentals of Aquaponics were practiced by the Indians more than 1,000 Years Back. Exotic farmers constructed land covered rafts called chinampas and found them at Lake Tenochtitlan. This had been this form of creativity that caused their rapid and great advancement for a culture. Further, the accelerated rise of food using the origin partially explains their capacity to encourage a sizable populated metropolis.

In Asia

South China and Thailand also practiced a sort of Aquaponics ancient in their history, even once they increased both fish and rice at precisely the same paddy areas. As in modern Aquaponics, the fish supplied compost to the rice and the plant origins spilled the drinking water.

The re-circulating Aquaponics System

Even though Aquaponics has ancient origins, the present-day Aquaponics system using closed-loop recirculation can be quite a recent innovation. The initial re-circulating Aquaponics program was Constructed from the 1970s, by Mark McMurty's, also a pupil of the New Alchemy Institute and a pupil of Vermont State University. Mark McMurty's approaches among many others acquired out of his job were used to generate food from lots of arctic third world states, however, the prevalence of Aquaponics from the U.S. and Canada is a 21st-century phenomenon.

The Way 21st-century Aquaponics Works

Aquaponics comprises several vessels. The boats are two purposes. 1 form of boat is meant to contain growing young fish along with the other type comprises plants that are growing. Plant containers have to be filled with technical Aquaponics networking, broadly speaking in the kind of rough clay chunks, or using pebbles. The plants have been implanted within this soilless medium. Vessels are linked to each other with a system of PVC plumbing pipes.

What Exactly Is Aquaponics Gardening?

Aquaponics is an innovative, noteworthy gardening strategy that unites traditional aquaculture (increasing aquatic creatures in tanks) with hydroponics (fostering plants from soil-free networking). At hierarchical surroundings, it increases both plants and fish within reciprocal environmental stability. Much like Hydroponics, the fastest-growing climbing systems do not require any dirt and alternatively use highly oxygenated, nutrient-rich H20.

Aquaponic gardening is extremely productive in growing organic veggies, fruits, fruits and increasing fish. More therefore, aquaponic approaches are just four to six times more efficient compared to ordinary households and require 90 percent less water. On a modest scale, they offer a cost-effective alternative to anyone and families seeking self-sufficiency.

On a bigger scale, they're a possible remedy to urban food insecurity. Not just is aquaponics on the list of very best gardening methods, nonetheless, it's the simplest solution to cultivate vegetables and herbs. Aquaponic systems are self-regulating: that you never need to wash your plants and also you don't need to completely clean out the aquarium. Irrespective of some basic maintenance activities, the only real thing left to complete is to nourish your fish and crop your vegetables!

The Aquaponics Cycle: The Way It Works

To put it differently, as water has been pumped out of the tank for your fish into the grow beds, so the fish waste has been switched into organic food for the plants. Your plant's in-turn wash, clean and then recycle the water for the fish. Because aquaponics can be shut and recirculating systems, it gives rise to naturally occurring bacteria (germs and microbes). These viruses and bacteria break down the fish waste (ammonium and nitrites) into compost for the plants (in the kind of nitrites).

When consuming the plants, plants filter out the water. The wash water then flows straight back in the volcano, giving your fish having a sterile and clean environment by which they can flourish. This expanding method is environmentally friendly, economical and natural. Employing natural bacterial cycles, it gets rid of all dependence on costly chemical fertilizers and water filters, and each whilst avoiding water wastage.

We'll enlarge on the countless advantages of all aquaponics in the second section, before continuing to the method that it is possible to begin in your journey to self-sufficiency and food liberty!

The Road of Water
Optional Filtration

Fish and Water waste are pumped out of the Aquarium through a pipe. The water might be passed by way of a more compact container comprising a loose fibre substance to get rid of excess solids until it flows to a system of plant containers.

This shouldn't be anything elaborate. Just a tiny polyester pillow stuffing at a skillet or jar works well. This gently filtered water then flows to the plant tanks. At the efficient, flooding drain systems the boats in which feature plants are gradually bombarded. If they get to the perfect degrees, a bell clot is integrated to empty the plants. Ergo that the plants aren't always immersed in water. As an alternative, they're watered and allowed to dry before being saturated back again.

This could be the natural cycle which many plants prefer. Once the water was filtered via a collection of plant cells it has been returned into the tank for your fish tank Vessel.

Variations

perhaps not many systems utilize bell siphons and also a flooding drain plan. Some systems leak constantly. Additionally, floating rafts could be incorporated into plants that want more watering, like the chinampas, these rafts might be set right on the top of the water of their tank for your fish.

Unlike chinampas, they feature no dirt. Aquaponics systems usually do not comprise any form of soil. There are many ways to look for an Aquaponics technique. Various kinds can work with various software and require varying degrees of experience and expertise.

The various angles of Aquaponics

An aquaponics system can be closed system permaculture using three components:

1. Fish

2. Plants
3. Compounds

These 3 components live work and side-by-side together to generate a mutually advantageous environment. This usually means that the appropriate balance of each is needed for the machine to stay fit and operational. Reaching this equilibrium, the pursuit which is a small addicting may be the most important objective of the aquaponics grower.

Plants love fish

The requirements of a plant are all simple: atmosphere, nutrients and water. When supplied with all these essentials, plants subsequently make use of the procedure for photosynthesis to convert surrounding light into sugar, which may be the foundation of vegetable thing.

Plants also expect a variety of nutrition in various quantities to photosynthesize successfully. The attractiveness of aquaponics is the fish could provide plants using those nutritional elements. It's no surprise that plants love to fish!

At a normal garden, animal manures may be utilized to supply plants with the nutrition they should cultivate. But these manures have to be properly used or processed to be able to generate the nourishment that they feature reachable.

At precisely the same style, an Aquaponics system operates when algae process fish waste, turning it to nitrates. This supplies the plants with all the nutrients that they have to cultivate at an extremely accessible type.

Even the aquaponics cycle begins if fish have been fedup, and also make waste. This waste is ammonia, which is fatal to fish at elevated levels. For that reason, nitrifying bacteria break it down to food. In consuming this specific food, plants filter out the water, that will be later coming back into the tank for your fish.

So how exactly can Aquaponics differ?

Many folks may item hydroponic and Aquaponics gardening has become alike, as well as in a few instances you can find similarities, however, there are undoubtedly significant differences between both techniques of gardening. Whereas the hydroponic garden can be a garden without dirt, the Aquaponics garden concentrates mainly on a symbiosis of nutrition between seeds and plants. Additionally, both approaches are extremely different from routine gardening too. At a Standard backyard, the Requirements of plants Are Usually provided for at a more ordinary manner:

- Sun provides light
- fire offers water and might be supplemented with irrigation
- S Oil stipulates an increasing media and also the nutrients that plants require

Growers can also enhance the soil and supply plants with additional nutritional elements with fertilizers and composts.

In a hydroponic garden, Alternatively, the rising environment is more regulated: -

* Plants have been grown in an inert press
* Water Is Continually cycled beyond plant origins, supplying hydration
* Nutrients are all provided in the biking water, also Result in Custom-made, compound combinations

The Benefits of hydroponics over traditional gardens comprise the enhanced hydration, in addition to the greater degree of management that farmers have finished theNutrients are readily available to plants. Nutrient solutions are customized to accommodate plant species along with their point in the development cycle, so which makes to more consistent returns and improved production all around.

Compared with organic gardening, aquaponics systems are Identical to hydroponics with a single crucial difference:

* Nutritional Elements Inside the cycle stems out of the bass, that creates waste That's subsequently converted to accessible plant foods from germs

Why choose aquaponics?

While aquaponics isn't quite as accurate as hydroponics when providing for particular harvest requirements, it is more economic: Aquaponics doesn't want costly chemical inputs, has less wastewater and gives that the grower with 2 plants (plants and fish) from precisely the same distance and inputs.

Aquaponics systems may also be exceptionally elastic, which makes them a suitable garden choice to get different ponds, places, spaces and requirements. The systems have been surprisingly straightforward to establish. They could be large or small, located inside or out, and certainly will support any range of aquatic animals and plant life species.

Aquaponics additionally interests people worried about food and health security. The vegetables and fish produced from the device are somewhat more reliable than those produced artificial, as aquaponics is inherently organic and also the grower knows what their manufacture has come in to contact. Also, fatty fish like carp and trout increased in an aquaponicssystem onto a controlled expired have elevated quantities of omega3 fatty acids, which are associated with cancer-prevention and different health and fitness benefits, compared to fish in commercial origins.

Chapter 2
Benefits and Kinds of Aquaponics

Recently, we're facing a requirement to develop more food on less land. Additionally, lots of forward-thinking individuals desire to ascertain individual, community and family food supply liberty. While commercial farming is based on GMOs, complex processing and transfer of food within large distances, so lots of men and women believe it's a lot more sensible for communities and families to produce their very own organic foods, even using heirloom seeds in the place of plants that are genetically engineered.

Manufacturing and Efficiency

Aquaponics is probably the most efficient method to elevate the most quantity of food in a little space. There are lots of explanations for why Aquaponics is indeed efficient.The very first rationale may be that the fish. A fish fed a pound of food can produce 1 pound of beef. In contrast, a cow needs to eat eight pounds of food to produce 1 pound of beef. As an extra plus, many species of fish will probably grow to acceptable ingestion size in six to eight weeks. The 2nd rationale Aquaponics produces therefore economically is a result of the superior fertilizer made by the fish that induces plants to grow faster and more prolifically. The 3rd rationale is a result of the efficient usage of water for a resource.

Powerful Usage of Water

Aquaponics is superior in water usage efficiency to classic gardening, hydroponics and aquaculture since it cannot waste or purify water. As alternative water is re-circulated and used again and again. The water that must be substituted would be that the water lost from the casual flow.

Self - sustaining

Aquaponics requires no fertilizer, no pesticides and nominal equipment. The sole completely crucial mechanical or electric component of the Whole system would be a small water pump capable of increasing a steady flow of warm water up a pipe to an elevation of approximately four or three feet above the surface.

A toaster pump or possibly a massive aquarium pump is adequate. The single other equipment which might be necessary can be that a heater, either for your water or at the green home.

Milwaukee Success

A forward-looking town, Milwaukee recognized the possibility of Aquaponics before a lot of those U.S A nonprofit company called Growing Electricity started Aquaponics Farming as early as 1993, which makes them even a pioneer within the specialty. Their metropolitan farm boasts the creation of a million pounds of food three acres a year, for example, 10,000 fish annually.

Many Food

Additionally, it is essential to be aware the Milwaukee's urban farm also produces various foods, not only 1 harvest. Their Aquaponics greenhouses grow around, in Milwaukee winters, even producing diverse foods such as Portobello mushrooms, many greens, greens, melons, lettuces and berries. They grow enough number to encourage people, having a widely varied balanced diet program.

Three Basic Kinds of Aquaponics Systems

When you will find virtually infinite variations of Aquaponics systems limited exclusively by the programmer's imagination, all Aquaponics approaches so far fall under three primary categories. It's also likely to construct systems that incorporate several of those sorts of systems in the same system. Again, experimentation and creativity may result in a good deal of versatility.

1: Nutrient Film System

The nutrient picture system doesn't incorporate planter vessels, either grow moderate or pebbles. As an alternative, a nutritional supplement picture system is made up of filters, and also a massive network of PVC pipes. Holes are drilled at the top of these PVC pipes and also a plant has been inserted into each hole. The circulation of water can be a steady demeanour, moving out of the tank for your fish throughout the system of pipes and straight back into the tank.

The single disturbance of the leak would be a filter tank to take out solids. That is critical to avoid a buildup of solids to the roots. The only real disadvantages with the technique would be the constant ingestion of plant roots and also the minimum requirement of filtering solids out.

2: Deepwater Raft System

Within this kind of system that the plants ride onto a foam raft drifting into the tank for your fish and also are found in nested containers. This notion is quite straightforward and will be incorporated readily. Regrettably, the Styrofoam raft will block oxygen which could otherwise permeate the water surface.

Furthermore, the water doesn't circulate thus aeration has been diminished. Additional aeration might be required if this really could be the only real Aquaponics facet of this system.

3: Flood and Drain Systems

Many Aquaponics farmers choose that the flood and drain procedure. This technique takes a system of grow bed boats linked to PVC pipes along with incorporating bell siphons for that intent of flood the grow beds into power and draining them back into the tank for your fish. Many discussions concerning kinds of Aquaponics systems come from variations from the setup of flooding drain techniques.

The CHOP system setup is your practical work-horse flooding and drains setup. CHOP is an acronym for Continuous height just one pump. The CHOP System includes growing beds of most the exact heights which aren't substantially lower or higher compared to tank for your fish. In a CHOP system, the septic tank, even if present, is normally under the beds.

Configuration design made by Travis Hughey in 2003. The system consists of drums and comes with a tactical height variant. The aquarium is at the end, whereas the beds that are growing, assembled of 2 parts of the similar plastic drum, which are greater compared to the fish water and usually hangover the surface of the fish container therefore that in case of an error all water drains into fish. A sump tank towers across the beds.

Customized Systems you will find lots of variations of those basic topics and thoughts. Systems using more than 1 pump may ease multiple fish tanks. Adding a sump tank may improve filtration and reduce solid waste from the computer system. Creating grow beds on distinct degrees or containing components from a raft or nutritional picture systems or alternative water fountain style elements canaffect an Aquaponics system both beautiful and complex.

Incorporating decorative aluminum tanks, perpendicular PVC planters, huge glass aquariums or cement fountains such as configurations with water drops could create Aquaponics beautiful. The invention of an original Aquaponics configuration is just constrained by the imagination. The majority of the pleasure of the Aquaponics system would be that the infinite options in design and configuration which encourage constant progress on systems that are already great.

Chapter3
Significant Elements, Things to Know Before You Start

While every method differs, and distinct fish and plants will have different requirements, you can find lots of concerns that are typical to each of the aquaponics setups. This chapter offers an overview of what exactly you want to learn before you start to construct your aquaponics program.

Water

Water is your lifeblood of this aquaponics system. It supplies the bond between plants, fish and bacteria, plus it really is water quality, first of all, that may impact their health insurance and functionality of this system. Even though 3 aspects of this machine have marginally distinct preferences, water payoff can be just a need shared with all.

Water sources

Water-quality is completely crucial for both plant and fish health. Rainwater is perfect for aquaponics techniques since it's one of the purest water available. But, it's crucial to try even rainwater, even as most areas of the whole world have problems with mild acid pollution and rains.

Water out of the rest of the sources needs to be broadly analyzed, and treated as mandatory, prior usage within an aquaponics program. Water out of mains systems has been treated, whereas water out of aquifers and bores could have elevated quantities of salts and minerals.

Frequent compounds utilized in sewage (tap) water

The majority of tap water from the Western World is chlorinated to kill germs and germs, which might be detrimental to humans. But, chlorine isn't only toxic for bacteria, but and to fish and lots of plants. If your plan is on using tepid to warm water in an aquaponics system, then it has to be treated. Chlorine dissipates in touch with the atmosphere, thus saving tap water at an open container for at least 4-8 hours, so you can guarantee it won't harm your ecosystem. Chlorine will exude more rapidly in the event the water is discharged.

The other frequent disinfectant applied in normal tap water is chloramine. Chloramine isn't quite as easy to remove as chlorine, also when it's employed in your town, you need to put money into sodium met bisulphite pills or a lively carbon dioxide filter.

Some states utilize alternative disinfectants to deal with drinking tap water, and it's crucial to learn what's employed in your town and also how to take care of it just before start your venture to aquaponics.

Water hardness and salinity

Along with disinfectants, water comprises numerous different minerals and compounds. These may stem from your water supply, like the stone of an aquifer, or become the consequence of further compound treatments. It's because of this it is essential to check your water origin thoroughly before use and consult with an expert to take care of some substantial impurities. Salinity is of specific concern, also water using higher salinity ought to be avoided in conventional aquaponics units.

Water that prevents soap from lathering or leaves a variety of lime can be known as "hard water". Hard-water contains 2 major triggers, both of which stem out of the stone the water has already established connection.Hard water could possess elevated quantities of sodium or elevated degrees of carbonates. Even though it's required to think about the mineral content of one's water supply, hard water can usually be employed without injury to the organisms within an aquaponics program.

pH levels

pH is the degree of acidity or alkalinity of a solution. While algae, fish and plants have slightly different pH preferences, broadly speaking it's always ideal to keep a supplementary system from the neutral to slightly acidic variety, with a pH of 6 - 7.5.

Microbial and bass activity can impact pH ranges, as can certain rising websites. The pH of something will most likely decrease more than requiring an alteration, however, major changes are due to issues. For that reason, analyzing the pH of your water resource as well as the device itself is excellent practice to prevent instabilities affecting receptor wellbeing.

Health and Safe Practices

Just like with any job, aquaponics units have several safety and health concerns that growers have to know about.

Employing ammonia as well as other compounds safely

Ammonia is toxic and may be kept safely at all moments. It shouldn't be inhaled, ingested or come in contact with skin. The use of gloves, goggles and a face mask is suggested. If contact with skin occurs, wash thoroughly with lots of soap and water. Get in touch with a physician or pharmacist information Centre instantly if inhaled or ingested.

Acids, bases as well as other compounds used within the observation and modification of the purification system pose similar risks to ammonia and ought to be treated equally.

Utilizing increasing media Safely

All climbing media is potentially detrimental. It's very important to have on a face mask if dry-handling, as sterile particles can lead to the lung disorder. Stone wool is very harmful, including particles very similar to fibreglass.

Safety measures for system handling

The most significant hazard posed by an aquaponics system would be electric safety. Ensure that your power source is grounded, and all of the wires are procured. Use trickle loops where appropriate rather than hang wires over water.

Wash your hands well with soap and warm water after handling machine components. The water in the machine can lead to skin irritation, particularly when pH or nutrient amounts are still out of the suggested range like in the starting phases of process biking. Aquaponics water can cause acute disease if ingested.

Hygiene

To prevent introducing potentially harmful compounds, which might influence system health in addition to the security of this manufacture, strict hygiene procedures must be followed closely.

Hands and equipment ought to be cleaned thoroughly before dealing with the body. All substances introduced into the device, like plants, feeds and creatures, should be out of the trusted, disease-free origin. Any substances of suspicious source, like seedlings raised in the dirt, ought to be sterilized before introduction. Gloves must be worn when handling bass. The system ought to be protected from potential culprits such as critters.

On account of the character of this system, contaminants like blood and body fluids must tend not to enter in to contact with it. This consists of stool and manures, even though their safe usage within different kinds of agriculture.

Healthful produce

Just like with any product, which increased in an aquaponics system may take potentially harmful pathogens. Risk is blindsided by preventing creation from coming in contact with this water and from then washing it thoroughly before ingestion.

When swallowing fish, never have any which reveal symptoms or signs of the disorder. Usually do not swallow fish increased in polluted water, and then purge fish feed prior usage. Purge fish at a light salt tub for 23 days until slaughter.

Beginning an Aquaponics system

Beginning an aquaponics unit isn't too easy as building something and adding plants and fish. Anyhow, you may possess a functioning system for weeks until it's prepared to populate. You must undertake system biking, and that's the practice to build a bacteria colony at an aquaponics unit, before adding fish, and sometimes plants that are even, to an individual system.

Bearing this measure from the practice of setting-up your unit is going to lead to the high priced deaths of plants and fish. Do not even consider fish till you've got your ammonia levels in check and you've got significant degrees of nitrates on the body.

Bacteria - Crucial little creatures

Aquaponics is dependent heavily onits job of bacteria to stop fish waste in reaching hazardous levels. Compounds hence create a critical connection between the aspects of the aquaponics ecosystem, so which makes it easy for plants to filter water from the computer system.

Additionally, 3 chief categories of bacteria are essential for the performance of an aquaponics system, and so can be usually known as the "bio-filter":

• Ammonia-oxidizing bacteria, switching toxic ammonia to nitrites;
• Nitrite-oxidizing bacteria that convert nitrites to nitrates, probably the many available types of nourishment to plants;
• Heterotrophic bacteria that break up a solid plant and fish transports into available micronutrients, which can be also crucial for plant development.

Even though all 3 types of bacteria are crucial to the performance of an aquaponics system, the most important focus is that the bacteria that treat nitrogen and ammonia. Even the ammonia-oxidizing and also nitrite-oxidizing bacteria are known to together as nitrifying bacteria, also, therefore, are the gap between your death and life of an aquaponics program. With no germs, the systems will immediately turn out to be toxic, leading to fish deaths.

Besides, healthy colonies of nitrifying and heterotrophic bacteria prevent the development of less beneficial bacteria, which may infect fish or plants, and harm the device, disturbing the critical balance of these device components.

Bacteria-friendly surroundings

it's quite crucial to produce an environment on your aquaponics system that's bacteria-friendly and can encourage the development of a bacterial colony that is healthy. This promotes nitrifying and heterotrophic bacteria that have similar ecological conditions, to replicate from the computer system.

Environmental requirements

Both the nitrifying and heterotrophic bacteria necessitate the subsequent elements.

A water temperature of between 60-85oF (15-30oC)

Compounds will endure temperatures out this range, however, their breeding and productivity decline. Because of this, it's very essential to track ammonia levels from the winter months, in recognized aquaponics components, because it's not unusual for low temperatures to inhibit bacterial exercise, leading to system toxicity.

A water pH of 6 - 7.5

Maybe not overly low or high, otherwise your living environment won't be fine for its bacteria, seeds and plants.

Protection from sun

Nitrifying bacteria are photosensitive, therefore protection against UV lighting is vital. Media beds offer you natural security, but care has to be drawn in systems that feature a biodegradable to be certain it is well-shaded. Also, the sun contributes to higher algae growth, which may inhibit bacterial work in addition to flushing system elements.

Substantial oxygen levels of elevated degrees of oxygen have been required for nitrifying bacteria to flourish. Luckily, plants and fish additionally prefer a well-oxygenated atmosphere.

An extra benefit of providing an abysmal surrounding is it is disliked by nearly all unwelcome bacteria that may otherwise purge an aquaponics system, like denitrifying bacteria and sulphatereducing germs, and each of which could make system requirements toxic to fish. Assuming that your own body is full of dissolved oxygen is perhaps one of the very dependable ways in which you can make certain that you're cultivating the ideal germs, but perhaps not the undesired types.

Exotic filter demands

A biofilter can be a massive tank that's intended to accommodate the nitrifying bacteria within an aquaponics unit (heterotrophic bacteria will naturally purge any regions where solid waste can be available, like underneath of fish aquariums, filters and also build beds). It's a dependence on NFT systems, also is a helpful addition to the majority of aquaponics units.

The Advantages of a Bio-filter have been twofold: it offers an Acceptable habitat for bacteria that are transmitted, permitting bigger colonies than are potential only in mature beds, and thus producing ammonia poisoning more improbable; also it permits for

The extra water from the machine, protecting bacteria and fish in the event of a plumbing malfunction.

A biofilter needs to offer the perfect habitat for bacteria that are transmitted, therefore they have to be vacuumed and opaque, as a way to shield bacteria from the sun. Biofilters must be well-aerated, also it's not unusual to situate an air stone within.

Nitrifying bacteria will expand on any surface, therefore the main intention of a biofilter would be to extend a great deal of area for the bacteria to colonize. This may contain a tank filled up with a few of those above growing websites (porous lava rock or enlarged clay beads operate especially well), using dyed plastic or Styrofoam packaging beads (large enough never to block filters or input the machine), commercially-produced "Bio-filter Balls" and on occasion despite having packs of some large-gauge plastic sheeting or mesh fabric. Any material which offers a distance for bacteria colonies to cultivate will probably get the job done.

Sourcing bacteria

Heterotrophic bacteria exist naturally anyplace and certainly, will populate a brand new aquaponics unit at adequate amounts that sourcing them is unnecessary.

Nitrifying bacteria exist naturally in warm water and atmosphere and certainly will purge a brand fresh aquaponics unit unassisted once procedure biking is started. But lots of fresh aquaponics growers source nitrifying bacteria externally. Remember that bacteria colonies aren't made, they also grow. For that reason, sourcing nitrifying germs only accelerates the practice of system biking marginally, it cannot worsen it.

Nitrifying bacteria might be obtained in two manners:

* Aquaponics, aquaculture and plant stores sell various "liquid" kinds of bacteria that are transmitted.
* Bio or water filter material in a balanced and mature aquaponics system, and sometimes an aquarium, may be utilized as a supply of bacteria that are transmitted.

Of those options, bottled bacteria might help establish a bio-filter rapidly, however,it is costly and will be hard to source. In case it may be determined that material by a proven system is disease-free, then this really may be the very best method to start procedure biking. But, counting upon natural and unassisted colonization is every bit as powerful in the long run.

System Cycling

System cycling may be the procedure for setting a new colony of nitrifying bacteria within an aquaponics unit. Even when bacteria can be sourced in an aquaponics store or existing method, biking will continue to be necessary to be able allowing bacteria to colonize the newest system in adequate amounts to guide fish.

Nitrifying bacteria replicate relatively gradually, and so the practice of system biking may occur between 14 days and two months, based upon the very first supply of bacteria along with ecological conditions like temperature. Many start aquaponics drinkers eventually get impatient, adding bass until the device biking is full. Since there are inadequate nitrifying bacteria to process most of their waste, these fish will more than likely perish and people that survive will probably be sick and stunted in their protracted exposure to elevated amounts of ammonia and nitrite.

System cycling is made up of gently adding ammonia into some brand new aquaponics unit. The system can be conducted, or so the water flow, as though the machine has been creating and complete, even though there aren't any fish or plants. As well as ammonia offers a food source of the bacteria that are transmitted and promotes the establishment of a bio-filter colony.

Sources of ammonia for system biking

Various resources of ammonia might be useful for procedure biking. Options range from the next.

Pure ammonia

In a few nations, it's likely to buy ammonia in hardware or even chemists. Ammonia might also be around as a cleanser and may be utilized to procedure cycle provided it doesn't include colourants scents or different additives.

Fish-food

New fish-food ground into a fine powder is also a relatively affordable ammonia supply for cycling.

Biological sources

Animal manures and obsolete urine may be applied as an ammonia supply, however, if be sterilized to make certain that unwelcome germs and bacteria aren't introduced into this device.

Fish

Fish transported in a very lower density 1 to 2 per 9 cubic feet (1 to 2 per M3) -- could be applied as the first supply of ammonia. Silk collar fish (transported at 5 to 10 per 9 cubic feet (5 to 10 per M3) as a result of their small size) usually are the most effective option as fatalities are high and those fish are not unlikely to thrive. But this origin makes it rather tricky to regulate ammonia levels from the body and also isn't suggested.

How to system cycle

Once the aquaponics apparatus is water and running stream is created, a little bit of ammonia is inserted into the machine daily. This ammonia supplies

The continuous food supply of that nitrifying bacteria and promotes the establishment of both colonies.

After adding ammonia at first, the objective is always to establish and keep a system-wide ammonia degree of over two minutes of a percentage (0.005percent). Degrees somewhat higher than that will likely soon be toxic to even nitrifying bacteria and require that the instantaneous dilution of plain water from the computer system.

Be aware that pure ammonia is offered in various strengths, or so the quantity added into this machine will count on the water amount of one's unit in addition to the concentration of one's ammonia resource. At a biking program, ammonia-oxidizing germs will purge the mosquito in the very first week, resulting in a growth of nitrates from water. After a week, the device will demonstrate either nitrites and nitrates, as clusters of nitrite-oxidizing bacteria become recognized.

After the device has ammonia and nitrite quantities of less than 0.00005 ounces per gallon (1 2 milligrams per litre) -- essentially, ammonia levels so reduced as to be immeasurable -- that the procedure biking method is complete. Compounds colonies are created and the machine is prepared for the accession of fish and plants.

Adding fish and plants

Even though they will probably not flourish, plants might be inserted into an aquaponics system before the ending of system cycling. Fish, alternatively, should just be inserted once biking is whole.

When you've finished the procedure biking procedure but are still not prepared to add fish, then a well-balanced degree of ammonia needs to be inserted into the device each day as if cycling. If that is failed, your cultivated bacteria colonies will immediately starve to departure and you'll need to begin with the procedure again.

Fish ought to be used gradually to some brand new siphoned apparatus, a couple at one time. Even in tiny amounts, fish are more very likely to create more ammonia compared to the bacteria colonies that are all familiar with processing. It'll choose the device several days to revive a balance and bring ammonia and nitrite levels straight back again to below 0.00005 ounces a quarter (1mg per litre) once of fish which were added.5.3 Tracking bacteria

Though a brown slime from the shrub filter or even onto different system surfaces is due to bacteria that are transmitted, it's not possible to assess the populace of the colonies on a house scale. As an alternative, bacteria are tracked through measurements of ammonia, nitrites and nitrates.

Nitrites and nitrates will just be found within an aquaponics system throughout the performance of bacteria that are transmitted, also in the event, a well-balanced ammonia and nitrite degree of below 0.00005 ounces per gallon (1mg per litre) is kept, it might be safely presumed that the bacteria on your system remains healthy and joyful.

Chapter 4
Which Fish to use and Other Key Decision to Make

Within this chapter, I will speak about the way to cultivate your garden's means to show poisonous ammonia into the compost called eucalyptus. We are going to discuss different kinds of nitrogen and also the way they affect fish therefore that you can stay away from killing your fish while the lawn is still maturing. This chapter covers how to make the dimensions to track your lawn's progress and how to correct your water to make the most of the fitness of your fish and plants.

Beneficial Compounds and the Nitrogen Cycle

Your plants need nitrogen to flourish. Nitrogen is a chemical essential for life in the world and also a crucial ingredient in protein. But although the atmosphere is mostly carbon dioxide, plants cannot make use of the nitrogen from the atmosphere. Ammonia is an application of nitrogen that originates out of fish waste, including draining fish, fish gillsfish and fish blossom.

But plants cannot utilize ammonia. Plants need saltwater, a form of nitrogen that's established out of ammonia from beneficial bacteria, to fuel their growth. Once you get a healthier population of those bacteria, your lawn should have the ability to transform ammonia out of the fish to saltwater to the plants.

The beneficial bacteria are too small to find, however, we can quantify whether they truly are from the garden by the total amount of ammonia, nitrite (an intermediate kind of nitrogen between nitrate and ammonia), and nitrate we all notice from the atmosphere. Later in the chapter, I will speak about the best way to execute the basic evaluations to assess the existence of these compounds.

As soon as an aquaponic garden is fresh, there's not anything from the water. As soon as we examine the water, then the outcome reveal is no ammonia, no nitrite, without a nitrate. We bring germs providing food. And the very first foods that they desire is ammonia.

Later in this chapter, I will speak about the way to present ammonia into your garden. After having a week or two longer, the ammonia levels will start to drop, and you'll begin to find out nitrite while in the computer system. This really is actually the signal that you own a little populace of these bacteria, called nitrifying germs, and that eat ammonia and also produce nitrite.

We are going to continue adding ammonia into the device to nourish the nitrifying bacteria, and also our evaluations will demonstrate that the ammonia is being converted into nitrite. After a week, the nitrite will start to disappear and we are going to observe chamomile. What this means is we've brought the following sort of bacteria. The bacteria, called nitrifying bacteria, eat nitrite and change it into saltwater, which is plant germ. For those who possess nitrifying and nitrifying bacteria present, the majority of people just refer to them as bacteria that are transmitted. The practice of developing the bacterial aspects of one's garden is known as cycling.

Cycling Your Own Garden

It is possible to merely put in fish into the brand new water into your tank for your fish and then plant trembling on your dirt rather than assess the ammonia, nitrite, and nitrate from water. But water chemistry has got an enormous effect on the overall health of your plants and fish.

It's worth some time to see the way one's body evolves with the years therefore that you may optimize your crop and maintain your plants and fish healthy. If you can immediately set a solid colony of bacteria that are transmitted, you're able to encourage more plants and fish on your aquaponics system. Let us speak about different kinds of nitrogen therefore that you can comprehend how each changes your plants and fish.

Fish Poison: Ammonia

To initiate the cycle, then you want to permit a great deal of ammonia to exist on your tank and then grow beds. Regrettably, this massive level of ammonia has the potential to kill your fish. It is possible to either utilize inexpensive fish whose potential departure you won't snore, or you'll be able to add ammonia with another procedure to cycle your system before adding live fish. The following are a few proven tactics to put ammonia in your garden to begin the cycling procedure. Ammonia. The very first means to bring ammonia would be to simply bring ammonia sulphate crystals or liquid ammonia that is pure. If you should be fine with chemistry, then you also can figure out the quantity of ammonia necessary to enhance the ammonia levels to 0.5 parts per million (ppm) or 0.5 mg per litre (mg/L).

If your chemistry is either rusty or if you fail to work out the potency of the services and products you're adding from the packaging, then you are going to have to check your water employing the processes discussed in this chapter. Carefully assess the ammonia and then add a bit at a time before the ammonia test kit provides you with a reading of 0.5 parts per million (ppm) or 0.5 mg per litre (mg/L).

Record just how much money which required. Insert the identical sum of ammonia every day and examine the concentration of ammonia and nitrite from the water. As ammonia levels grow towards 5 ppm, you should start seeing nitrite. Once nitrites appear, halve the quantity of ammonia you are adding and begin analyzing nitrates. Once ammonia and nitrite levels have fallen to zero and nitrates are emerging, it's safe to bring fish.

Ammonia generally seems to become the quickest solution to set a solid colony of beneficial bacteria, however, it could be challenging to come across pure ammonia without even added detergents or perfumes. When the ammonia is either coloured or if it foams whenever you shake the jar, then do not use it.

If the tag states it is clean ammonia, pristine ammonia, 100 percent ammonia, or Pure Ammonium Hydroxide, it's nice to use. Most stores sell the foamy perfumed material, however, you ought to find a way to come across pure ammonia in professional cleansing stores or hardware stores.

Fish. Fish add ammonia into an own tank anytime they breathe, flake, or even feces. Gold-fish makes a whole lot of ammonia inside their water and can endure more ammonia compared to some other forms of fish. For all these reasons, they're a terrific fish to utilize because you develop ammonia levels on your tank. Still another option will be by using a little populace of fish, also referred to as fingerlings, of one's planned fish species. The truth is that they have been smaller, younger fish means that they won't deliver too much ammonia being the complete people of fish that is mature. Less ammonia means that the smaller population of beneficial bacteria, however,also, entails every person fish isn't ingesting up to poison with every gill-full of plain water.

Organic thing. Rotting organic matter emits ammonia. Some people will just set a dead fish two in their tanks to create the very first ammonia blossom. As the fish are dead, there is no worrying about if the ammonia from the water may kill them. Still another organic supply of ammonia is obsolete urine, known throughout preindustrial times aslant. It had been broadly used back for cleanup, improving awareness of dyes from the material, and flavouring ale. Lant wouldbe fermented for monthly or two longer in a container to enable the ammonia to grow precisely. Preventing bottles of pee, however, is typically not the cup of java. To quote the majority of my pals,"Eeew!"

Oxygen-Binder: Nitrite

Nitrite is not as toxic to fish compared to ammonia, however, it could still kill your fish because thereby prevents blood from consuming oxygen. The kinds of bacteria which convert ammonia to nitrite are happiest and most successful involving 70° along with 80°F.

As temperatures drop below 50°F or grow above 100°F, these bacteria will quit feeding ammonia and certainly will perish. Since jelqing prevents fish bloodstream out of consuming oxygen, nitrite poisoning is also known as a brown blood disorder. Elevated degrees of nitrite damage your fishes' nervous programs, livers, spleens, and kidneys. Even lower doses could cause longterm damage. When nitrate levels are very high, fish could suffocate even though there's loads of oxygen from water.

People with decorative fish aquariums incorporate methylene blue into some tank to further enhance the power of fish to transport oxygen into their bloodstream, hence preventing fish deaths. Even though it isn't yet determined if methylene blue is toxic to plants and foodfish, to maintain the flip side, do not put it into an aquaponics system.

These nitrite concentrations are only going to endure a couple of weeks, and normally will not be enough to kill the couple small fish you'd possess in a brand new aquaponics program.

Plant Fertilizer: Nitrate

Nitrate is precisely what you really would like. Nitrate is also the principal source of nutrition for the plants and also will be extracted nicely by fish at concentrations far higher than nitrite or ammonia.

The germs which eat nitrite are additionally equal between 70° and 80°F, plus so they can expire when the temperature falls below 50°F or climbs above 100°F. You are never going to need to socialize with bacteria that are transmitted. They'll appear and perform their job, just like a quiet, invisible workforce.

Provided that ammonia and therefore are not quite zero and nitrate exists, the bacteria come set up and doing their job. If your machine is perfectly balanced, then the plants will probably soon be swallowing the saltwater, and that means you could get readings near zero to ammonia, nitrite, and nitrate.

Additional Suggested Additives

Aquaponics approaches make use of the output signal from the fish, hence any nourishment found from the fish will sooner or later wind up on your garden. There are just two supplements, however, that the typical aquaponics gardener may wish to own onhand.

Adding Iron to Green Plants

Most fish-food does not contain substantial levels of iron. A scarcity of iron can prevent the plants from producing adequate chlorophyll for photosynthesis, the process of converting sunlight into energy. Whenever your plants do not possess enough iron, then their leaves will get pale. The type of iron that you would like touse is chelated iron, also a powdered form that dissolves readily in water.

Metal rust and iron won't add the type of iron that your plants may utilize. A tsp of chelated iron to get a 200-gallon tank needs to create your plants grow lush, green development. Do not worry if leaves which had been yellowish remain like that --consider the brand new growth.

If you don't observe the green growth you would like, wait a week or two longer before adding more iron. A lot of iron may damage your fishso it is much better to own marginally yellowed leaves compared to fish that is damaged.

Employing Norwegian Kelp to Insert Vitamins

Seaweed or kelp can be an abundant supply of nutritional supplements, and parasitic kelp is very abundant with the broad array of nutritional elements required by plants. Maxicrop and Seasol are normal industrial brands of Deadly kelp extract readily available in the USA and Australia. Norwegian kelp seaweed comprises more than 60 nutrientsvitamins and beneficial enzymes. These nutrients include potassium and calcium, neither of which will be often found in fish food. The chamomile infusion is likely to create your water turn into a rusty color initially. You shouldn't be alarmed--it will not seem to disturb the fish or plants.

Altering pH

pH is a measurement of if the water is acid, neutral, or alkaline. Your plants and fish will probably soon be most moderate if your water is neutral (that a pH of 7.0) or slightly acidic (a pH between 6.0 and 7.0). It's very good to check on pH at every month, as rain, plain tap water, and also the bacteria on your own body can change the pH of one's garden. If your water is now not impartial, you'll find a couple of straightforward techniques to reestablish the balance between acidity and alkalinity in your garden.

Reducing pH

In case your water is more alkaline, with a pH above 7.5, then you're want to cut back pH. The very best method to try this fast will be always to bring acid. The very best sorts of acid to utilize are lipoic acid, also called muriatic acid. It's possible to discover muriatic acid at the pool distribution part of your community hardware shop. Work with a plastic spoon to bring a little quantity acid to some of this grow mattress from the standpipe.

Like that the acidity becomes diluted with all of the water draining out of the grow bed until it's reintroduced into the aquarium, preventing concentrated acid by coming into touch with your fish. Some individuals advocate lemon juice or apple ciderbut it will take large amounts of either of those juices to greatly alter your pH. Aquarium supply stores take a compound referred to as pH Down, nevertheless also the pH Down employed in Zinc comprises sodium, which could damage plants such as berries.

Increasing pH

Once I started doing aquaponics I couldn't imagine the need to maximize my pH. The water that I draw out of the tap would be extremely plump along with also my original develop mattress used river stones which retained my pH quite high. However, at a garden, the bacteria produce small quantities of acid since they transform ammonia to saltwater, in order time you may require to add something to cancel acid.

Hydroxide or even carbonate/bicarbonate chemicals of potassium and calcium will be the recommended means to maintain the garden from becoming overly acidic. Not only will those maintain your water impartial, but the potassium and calcium are also all crucial nourishment for healthy plants. Stir a small quantity of these dyes into social networking at which water comes into your kitchen beds, or scatter the powder in your filter in case you never utilize press.

Focus on small levels and quantify your water that the very next day to observe the affect pH. as time passes you'll become accustomed to the sum you want to grow your platform to acquire the desirable effects. An easy, natural means to maintain your garden from becoming overly acidic would be always to add crushed eggshells or even sea-shell grit to some large part of your garden. The cubes will quit dissolving whenever your pH climbs above 7.5, therefore there's minimal threat of earning your pH too large.

Assessing your system

when you're growing inland, analyzing one's body isn't simple. You've got to dig various chapters of one's garden, permit the dirt to wash, then purchase a soil evaluation kit or ship it off into a laboratory. However, as an aquaponic garden employs water, you may utilize the very simple evaluation kits manufactured for aquariums.

The conventional fresh-water master evaluation kit sells for approximately $20 and comprises all you will need to measure pH, ammonia, nitrite, and simmer tens of thousands of times. Along with the dimensions, you'll be able to make with a normal aquarium evaluation kit, so I would advise that you measure and set temperature. You might even measure dissolved oxygen (DO) in the event you're concerned with whether your fish will be receiving enough oxygen to keep healthy.

It's a fantastic idea to list these dimensions in a log, for example exactly what you've done to your own body and what exactly you find about your fish and plants. I suggest analyzing daily for your initial couple of weeks, then a week or twice whilst the water chemistry dissipates.

Assessing Your Own Water Chemistry

The cheap evaluation kits that I urge comprise glass tubes with caps and squeeze bottles of compounds. The conventional aquarium test kit does not support the compounds for analyzing dissolved oxygen. Salifert supplies a dissolved oxygen test kit that's cheap and works like the evaluation kits for pH, ammonia, nitrite, and nitrate.

Before beginning, rinse your tubes out. I fill out the tubes around 50% put the cap, shake vigorously, and then discard the water. If I am unsure the tube is sterile, I replicate this measure. Add water to the fill line indicated from the glass pipes. While I over-fill, I shake the tube in my expansion bed to generate a couple of drops fly outside. Through the years you will receive very proficient at fast becoming the degree exactly perfect.

Insert the suggested range of drops out of the squeeze bottle and check the colouring of their water against a card to ascertain the water chemistry. Make use of the plastic caps which include the evaluation kit to limit the evaluation vials rather than using your palms. Your palms could pose contaminants that may impact the dimensions.

Additionally, some chemicals employed in the evaluation kit aren't skin-friendly. Listed here will be the normal directions for measuring each significant facet of chemistry. Testing pH is fast and easy. Assessing ammonia, nitrite, and nitrate takes five minutes each vial. If you do all of them at precisely the same period, it requires approximately five minutes to try your water.

Follow the following steps to try pH:

1. Insert 5 millilitres (ml) of plain water in the own system to a fresh test vial.
2. Add 3 drops of pH evaluation treatment for the vial (5 drops in the event the high-ph test solution).
3. Cap the vial and invert a couple of times. Colour grows instantly.
4. Compare the tone of the water from the vial into the guide card which includes the evaluation kit.
5. Record the pH primarily based on your quote of their ideal colour match.

Follow the following steps to try ammonia (NH3):

1. Add 5 ml of plain water in the own system to a fresh test vial.
2. Add 8 drops out of the very first ammonia evaluation jar into the vial.
3. Cap the vial and shake for 5 minutes.
4. Add 8 drops out of the 2nd ammonia evaluation jar into the vial.
5. Cap the vial and shake 5 minutes.
6. Wait five minutes to colour to grow.
7. Record the ammonia concentration at mg/L or even ppm based in your quote of their ideal colour match.

Follow the following steps to try nitrite (NO2):

1. Add 5 ml of plain water in the own system to a fresh test vial.
2. Add 5 drops out of the nitrite test jar into the vial.
3. Cap the vial and shake for 5 minutes.
4. Wait five minutes to colour to grow.

5. Record the nitrite concentration in mg/L or even ppm based in your quote of their ideal colour match.

Follow the following methods to try nitrate (NO3):

1. Add 5 ml of plain water in the own system to a fresh test vial.
2. Add 10 drops out of the very first nitrate evaluation jar into the vial.
3. Cap the vial and shake for 5 minutes.
4. Shake the 2nd jar of nitrate evaluation solution for 30 minutes.
5. Add 10 drops out of the 2nd nitrate evaluation jar into the vial.
6. Cap the vial and shake 60 minutes.
7. Wait five minutes to color to grow.
8. Record the nitrate concentration in mg/L or even ppm based in your quote of their ideal color match.

Assessing Dissolved Oxygen

In case your fish have been gulping at the top like they cannot get enough oxygen, then you will wish to try the dissolved oxygen on the body to be certain they will have sufficient oxygen in your water. Should they have sufficient oxygen, then it may be any other problem with all the water, for example as excessive jelqing, and a water shift of about 25 percent is inorder.

Dissolved oxygen is measured in the exact components as the nitrogen chemicals, in mg/L or ppm. The directions are much like one other vial-based evaluation kits:

1. Add 5 ml of plain water in the own system to a fresh test vial.
2. Add 5 drops out of the very first jar of oxygen evaluation solution (O2-1) and then swirl lightly for 20 minutes. Don't shakethis can alter the oxygen of their water.
3. Add 6 drops out of the next bottle of oxygen evaluation solution (O2-2) and then swirl gently for 15 minutes. Allow the solution to stand for 1 second.
4. Add 6 drops out of the next jar of oxygen evaluation solution (O2-3) and swirl to get 20 minutes. Let me stand 30 minutes.
5. Record the dissolved oxygen concentration at ppm based in your quote of their ideal colour match.
6. Record water temperature, since water temperature, affects the most potential amount of pressurized oxygen.

Keep your body pH between 6.0 and 7.0 keep your plants and fish healthy. Watersoluble (chelated) iron along with chamomile infusion may add nutrients, not within fish food. Quantify your water chemistry each day before all of the nitrogen is turning up as nitrate as opposed to ammonia or nitrite. Carry on reading to quantify your water chemistry weekly or monthly, at least.

Chapter 5
Which Plants Grow Best

Just about any plant that you grow in a standard garden can grow within an aquaponic garden, especially if you're employing media-filled beds. There are a couple of slight differences between growing within an aquaponics garden and growing in a conventional dirt garden. For the large part, but you can study the broad experience base of classic gardening. If you do not have a shelf filled with art novels, let's cover some basics in this matter.

Working with a Planting Guide

Planting guides help do you realize what veggies grow well in the community area so when you ought to plant them. These manuals are frequently available from local gardening classes and agricultural extension services, and organizations that sell plants. Information usually comprised in planting guides comprises the following:

- Distance between crops for every single harvest
- Approximately Yield per average row
- Just how many row ft you Want to feed Somebody
- The Sum of seed (or quantity of crops) you desire per row
- If to plant seeds or reevaluate transplants
- when You're Able to anticipate to crop every harvest

If your neighborhood adventures are chilly, this guide will let you know that the normal date of the last killing frost in spring and the date of the first killing frost in autumn. For those who have use of the world wide web, there's just a good internet site made by Kristee Rosendahl called smartgardener.com.

Smart gardeners enable you to produce a photo of one's garden, pick exactly what plants to utilize, and set them in your garden to prevent them projecting color in your neighbors, and the website sends you emails with advocated activities. The only real bad thing concerning Smart gardener is that I cannot switch tabs off for all your heaps of chores soil-based anglers must accomplish (like weeding, watering, and also interrogate dirt).

For those who own a tablet or smartphone computer device, you can find numerous gardening programs that will assist you to organize your garden, which makes the job of preparation, planting, and harvesting your lawn easy and enjoyable.

Famous gardening has been popularized in the USA by Mel Bartholomew together with his Square-foot Garden method. He urged little scale beds by which a gardener may easily get to the plants without being forced to step in the garden. At Square Foot Gardening, the garden is broken up using a grid, clearly marking each square foot. The suggested range of desirable plants is subsequently planted in each square. You can find over 100,000 anglers employing the square-foot Garden system, helping to make it simple to locate accessories such as supports and trellises for climbing plants. Aquaponic gardens are great for intensive gardening seeing as you're delivering nutrient-rich water to your plant origins and just require enough room around each plant so that it can grow correctly.

Strictly Summer Plants

All these are plants that cannot withstand cool weather and so are killed by frost. They love the heat of summer and tend to be known as very tender plants. You may normally wish to start these plants inside as seeds a handful of months before the past proposed frost. Following 3 weeks, they'll soon be large enough to safely plant in your backyard.

Tomatoes

Tomatoes are yummy and filled with Vitamin C and also, therefore, are the most used of their nightshade veggies. These certainly were on the list of veggies that the Aztecs cultivated. Tomatoes grow in bushes or vines. The bush forms are known as jelqing, meaning they reach a certain height and also quit growing. As the bushes are quite streamlined, these sorts of edible plants usually do not desire pliers or trellises.

Tomatoes may occupy plenty of space, however, should precisely be trellised, a lone plant should require no greater than the usual 2-foot from 2-foot location. Vine tomato forms are called indeterminate because they keep climbing until cool weather destroys the entire plant. Because the vine grows, mature leaves will wither and perish. It's beneficial to develop a crate or trellis for all these vines. Tomatoes are Self-pollinating, meaning that they can produce fresh fruit out of one blossom without counting upon end, insects, or individual intervention to permit the pollen to make it to the reproductive section of the plant.

Many indoor manufacturers love to guarantee pollination by tapping on the blossoms or having a brush to be certain that the pollen out of the blossom reaches on the reproductive section of the blossom.

Peppers

Sweet peppers and chilli peppers were domesticated 6,000 decades ago at Central America and so we're on the list of foods Christopher Columbus delivered to Europe after his trip to North America. Peppers are a portion of the nightshade family. They can do well planted near other nightshade plants in addition to near onions, celery, carrots, and ginger.

It's ideal to maintain berries as well as other nightshade veggies from legumes, corn, wheat, and plants from the cabbage family. If you reside in a mountainous region or when pepper plants grow overly large to encourage themselves, then you also can drive a yard-long bet into the floor and connect the stem into it using something soft, such as old pantyhose. Peppers are all Self-pollinating, which makes these a fantastic plant to get the internal garden.

You're able to harvest peppers whenever they continue to be green or wait till they turn reddish or yellowish, once they've significantly more vitamin C.

Eggplant

Eggplant is just another person in the nightshade popular among anglers. The plant is indigenous to India, also spread into Europe throughout the Dark Ages. Each plant needs to produce 2 to three meals, which are ordinarily purple with white flesh. Eggplant needs to be chosen while they're glistening.

Once they become lighter and dull in color they are overripe and so are sent right to the compost bin. Melons such as cantaloupe and watermelon started from Africa, however, their candy flesh is now a favorite food around the whole world.

Melons

Grow on vines with large leaves and may occupy plenty of room when left to grow across the soil. In tiny gardens, melons might be trained on trellises to optimize production from the little space offered. Melons aren't Self-pollinating, counting upon insects for pollination.

Warm Weather Plants

Warm weather plants do not like frost but could frequently be seeded or transplanted to the garden when the danger of frost is past, even when current weather continues to be trendy. Additionally, you will observe these plants called tender.

Squash

From the ceaseless categorization wars of vegetables and fruit, botanists will telephone fruits. However, most cooksparents and kids contemplate skillet to be veggies. Squash, such as tomatoes and berries, Started from the Americas. Summer squash has tender skins and ought to be eaten through the hot season by which they're grown.

Winter squash can continue many weeks following the fall crop; they maintain well for use after winter due to these tough skins. Squash plants occupy a large quantity of space per plant--I'd love to boost my squash plants to accomplish their climbing out my greenhouse, though their origins remain in my high-rise beds.

The berry will release both female and male blossoms. You're able to tell the man blossoms due to their stems are directly and lanky. The stalks of these female blossoms are curved, and also these stalks will grow into the skillet when the flower is pollinated. The large gold pumpkin blossoms might be ready as food in an assortment of ways, that will be very good once you are up against heaps of man squash blossoms and almost no one of those female pumpkin blossoms which have potential to eventually become squashes. My preferred skillet blossom recipe is skillet blossom tempura, where the blossoms are dipped in a light batter and also deep-fried.

Green Beans

The most popular green-bean was just another crop Columbus attracted to Europe in 1493. Green beans have been classified as bush legumes or stick beans. Bush beans grow fast and may produce their legumes within a two- to one-hundred span. You want to begin sequential plantings to continue to keep a steady source of legumes coming throughout the length of the growing season.

Pole beans take longer to grow but may continue to produce legumes before autumn frosts kill this plant. Pole beans are best grown a vertical service, which is quite a simple as a series hanging out of a solid pub overhead. Bean plants are deemed green algae because they consume oxygen from the atmosphere and improve the earth by which they rise. Green beans have been considered bunny legumes since they are sometimes eaten at the pod. You might even grow shell legumes, the countless of bean varieties which are thought to be taken off after the beans have been older.

Sweet Corn or Maize

Corn has been originally the standard name for cereal crops such as barley, wheat, barley, and rye. The glowing yellowish grain we think about as corn has been introduced into Europe by Columbus and fellow explorers. The corn plant produces a tall stem that yields 2 into three ears. Because corn wants a great deal of nitrogen to flourish, it's normally spaced one foot apart. However, when the corn comes with nitrogen that is adequate, the potential within an aquaponics system, corn could be implanted as tightly as every 6 inches, or even four plants per square foot. Indigenous Americans would plant corn, beans, and squash together and known as those plants since the 3 Sisters.

The beans could pump dirt into the ground. The corn could offer a tall stem for its bean plant to grow, and also the squash leaves will shield the earth like mulch, with all the prickly hairs onto the vines deterring insects. After the plants grown, dishes mixing corn and legumes provided whole nourishment, reducing the requirement to improve domestic animals.

Cool-Weather Plants

Lots of popular garden plants will neglect during the heat of the summer. All these cool-weather plants, or semi-hardy plants, fared most useful while in the cool of spring and autumn. Using an aquaponics system that bathes the origins in heating, such semi-hardy plants may be increased through the entire summer except at the hottest climates.

Beets

Beets were likely strewn across the Mediterranean Sea until they propagate into ancient Babylon and China. We usually think about this candy, red root vegetable whenever folks discuss beets, however, the leaves will also be quite decent to eat. Beets may be reapplied 2 to 3 weeks until the last spring freeze and may endure being sown upto two weeks until the first killing frosts of collapse. The leaves are edible and create a brilliant addition to raw a yummy stirfry. At a brand new media-based aquaponics system, the origin of the beet may not develop.

However, once a machine continues to be a year to grow, you ought to be in a position to get Beetroots from plants. The crown of this origin will start to protrude from the increasing medium, providing you with a good notion of the magnitude of this origin. Don't hesitate to pull on the beet upto test you could always put it in the grow bed in case you never desire to eat it nonetheless.

Beetroots usually are prepared by massaging whole for 4-5 minutes, then yanking on-off the skin. Pickled beet eggs are a household favourite, a recipe that makes vivid and yummy utilization of this glowing reddish liquid left from massaging the beets.

Carrots

The lettuce is indigenous to both Europe and southwestern Asia. Both greens and also the origin of the carrot are all still edible, although the origin is the percentage the majority of people are utilized to ingestion. Carrots do not transplant well and require quite a very long time to germinate, however, they are sometimes implanted a couple of weeks until the last spring freeze as soon as 14 weeks before the first autumn.

Carrots require a foot of grow bed thickness to cultivate a nice root. Picking a medium is going to impact on just how directly the origins grow. Or you may grow around Parisian carrots which grow fast and do not require much grow bed thickness. Carrots are an excellent harvest to plant in the autumn to harvest from the winter. The chilly winter leaves whites candy, which makes for a delicious homegrown cure you can not buy from the stores.

Leafy Greens Leafy greens identify to all of the salad greens, for example, leaf lettuce, head lettuce, chard, and mustard. There are approximately several million species of plants with leaves that are edible, also within each species, there maybe tens of thousands of species. Beets are some particular, many species, though many folks do not think about it for a leafy green tea. Lettuce is your green people think about this particular category. It had been cultivated in Egypt and spread into Europe and the United States. It's currently eaten worldwide.

Some forms of leafy greens, such as iceberg lettuce, are also incredibly low in nutrition. However, other varieties could contain substantial levels of Vitamin C, especially once they're young.

Leafy greens

Grow best in cool weather, even where the cold prevents the plant from thriving. In hot weather, leafy greens can bolt, or blossom and go to seed. Once the plant is permitted to blossom, the many leafy greens eventually become bitter and tough.

Cold weather Plants

Coldweather or rugged plants may frequently be implanted outside a few weeks until the last frost of spring and might also be sown an additional time as autumn approaches. These plants can don't flourish from the heat of summer, in an aquaponics method. It can be possible to cultivate these plants throughout cold temperatures below a minimal hoop house or apartment with a row cap. Several of those plants may even survive freezing problems.

Cabbage as well as other Brassicas

Cabbage, as well as some other members of the brassica family, might be increased in cold weather. Kale is a favorite brassica since it's very full of vitamins and minerals that will assist in preventing canceras can lots of veggies at the brassica family. Bok choy is just a part of the cabbage family used usually in Asian cooking. The sharp leaves and stalks are cut and found in a stirfry. When increased in proper terms (early spring or autumn), bok choy can grow the moment 3-5 days' later seedlings emerge. The simplest brassica to cultivate could be your fact that overburdened. Radishes can grow in just fourteen days after seedlings appear. Lots of find raw radishes to become sour, however, they're flavorful when simmered at a small covering of plain water onions, salt, and pepperand then topped with a generous dollop of butter.

Peas

Peas are white round veggies that come in a pod. The first signs of humans using peas have been found around the Fertile Crescent, nearby the time when humans began to cultivate food as opposed to just collect it. Peas are a fantastic source of vegetable protein, also fresh beans out of the home garden might be quite so sweet that kids treat them like candies. There is certainly a huge array of legumes, letting you pick plants that suit your gardening personality (dense plants, vining plants, climbing plants), colour taste (purple, green, yellow) and preference (out of stir-fried snowpeas into mushy peas and sausage). The custom of eating beans in the pod was an imperial trend in the 1600s. Therefore, once you consume fresh peas in the garden, it is possible to truly say you're eating like a king.

Mâche

Mâche might well not be recognizable to the majority of modern anglers since it's slow to older and cannot be easily replicated using machines. However, the majority of folks have been aware of mâche with its alternative name, rapunzel.

Rapunzel was the yummy plant from the goat's backyard that enticed a pregnant peasant, that was made to offer her up golden-haired baby in charge. Mâche can also be called lamb's lettuce, field salad, and corn salad as it's so commonly found in areas. Mâche grows rampant in many parts of Europe, North Africa, western Asia, along with the two Atlantic and Pacific coasts of the Americas.

The imperial gardener of King Louis XIV introduced mâche into the Earth, also it had been grown commercially from London in the following years before the industrial era made additional veggies cheaper. Mâche can suffer freezing circumstances, even though it's going to do even better if given any protection against this weather. Mâche is considerably more wholesome than most conventional greens, using more vitamin C, vitamin B vitamins, antioxidants, vitamin E, also omega3 efas compared to just lettuce. Like most of the leafy greens, mâche tastes great whether it's chosen before blossoms appear.

Spinach

Spinach disperses from Asia all through Europe across the period of the Crusades, where it became so famous since among those few plants which could rise fast in spring throughout Lent, the 46 days before Easter Sunday when Christians constitute meat. The earliest written reference to spinach is within China, where lettuce has been understood as the "botanical vegetable" Now China produces 85 percent of most spinach grown on the planet.

Spinach is full of antioxidants and nutrients and research is continually turning new reasons individuals ought to put in spinach into our diet plans. Boiling spinach may remove a number of the nourishment, however, microwaving spinach doesn't impact nutrient levels just as much better. There are a couple of contamination loopholes between spinach, but those loopholes were due to pollution because of rampant fish and mass creation, neither that will occur with plants increased into the aquaponics system

Beyond Garden veggies

it's possible to grow significantly more than veggies in your garden. In reality, it could be less painful to simply set the few plants which do not flourish in overburdened systems. Listed below are a couple of kinds of plants you may be thinking about adding to your own body.

Herbs

Herbs will be the spice of life. It's excellent to have the ability to nip down to the garden and gather fresh herbs to season meals or garnish your plate. You pay a cent for them from the shop however they continue growing in your garden, readily replacing the pieces you slough off at only a matter of a couple of days.

Basil is just about the herb that delivers one of the most value if you're thinking about devoted to capsule production to make a little bit of cash on the medial side. Basil grows fast and will be propagated through cuttings very readily.   Simply snip excess branches off and then put them into the grow bed into the origin and then create a new plant.

I'll frequently cut a slit up the middle of the woody stem simply to grow the total amount of drinking water and nourishment that the cutting may get before the origins shape. Mint is 1 herb to cultivate using care. Mint grows sharply, and its origin systems may very quickly overpower different plants at the same bed. I like carrying several branches from the mint, then stripping the leaves off, and then steeping them in warm water to give fresh mint tea.

Trees

I had been curious when I saw people climbing banana trees, papaw trees, and even citrus trees inside their neighboring gardens. I had always believed the tree's root system was similar to an undercover mirror of its above-ground division system.

Unlike some innocent understanding, a clear vast majority of tree roots will stay in the upper 2-3 feet of the bottom, therefore it is not a dreadful hardship to get a tree to accommodate into the boundaries of an increased bed. But if you want to build trees, then you might choose to make use of an increased mattress which is significantly more than merely a 12 inches (300 millimeters) deep.

Flowers

It's not uncommon to plant marigolds within an aquaponics garden because marigolds repel most common garden insects. However, you're able to plant different blossoms too, like the Vinca I slid in my Windowfarm.Because aquaponics has primarily been dedicated to food output, there's relatively little info regarding growing flowers. Just about all varieties of blossoms can flourish at a pH assortment of 6.0 to 7.0. If you like flowers, I invite you to experiment to understand how your favourite blossoms do within an aquaponics garden in contrast to the way exactly they grow in dirt.

Duck-weed

You and that I will most likely not grow duck-weed to our dishes. However, this high-protein, the high-tech plant creates fantastic food for fish that eat plants. Many aquaponics anglers incorporate a shallow tank designed for growing duckweed to nourish into their bass.

Duckweed is a little floating plant, even with a little root which goes on to the drinking water. Duck-weed floating about nitrate-rich water will often twice every day or two through the summer. The rich food may be fed directly into the fish or suspended for days after the cold and short days make it difficult to cultivate much of anything.

Extending Aquaponics into Plants in Soil

I like the concept that my plants and fish make an entire mini-ecosystem. But despite my excitement for aquaponics, you can find a few garden plants which simply do not work nicely in aquaponics.

Two plants that spring into mind are blueberries and potatoes. Collars can grow in aquaponics procedures, however, they fared better in the dirt. Blueberries, alternatively, require soil having a pH of 4.5 to 5.0, which will be overly acid for fish along with the majority of other plants.

That you never have to leave favourite garden plants to resign to only growing such plants at a standard dirt garden. You're able to utilize water from the aquaponics system to water and purify dirt gardens.

Wicking Beds

Wicking beds are all dirt plots that break at the top of a reservoir of drinking water. The reservoir is made utilizing some form of waterproof fabric, such as vinyl sheeting, plastic bins ceramic or ceramic baths. At a low-tech daybed, the reservoir is full of massive rock material, such as gravel. The desirable thickness of dirt is shovelled in on top of this gravel. Some people stink a pipe so that they can examine the thickness of water from the reservoir having a pole. The others are going to divide the dirt out of the stones with a coating of geotextile, someone of a range of synthetic fabrics made specifically for keeping soil silt. Geotextiles might be either woven or nonwoven, also you might have observed them nearby construction websites, where they're utilized to decrease the quantity of dirt and sand on neighbouring roads.

The reservoir is full of overflow water out of the aquaponic system, and also the moisture and nutrients naturally travel to the ground overhead, especially as roots grow into the rugged reservoir. Pure naturally travels to the dirt overhead, especially as roots grow into the rocky reservoir. The Buster brothers telephone their own idea Worldwide Buckets, they promote via YouTube along with also their site, globalbuckets.org. Once they learned that plastic sheeting is considered very valuable in certain states that sailors do not wish to cut holes in the inner skillet, Grant and Max embarked on a Garbage Gardening job to generate gardens out of things considered crap even at the growing world. Because they explain, "Roots just require three crucial items: air, water, and nutrition." Sounds familiar to an aquaponic gardener!

Smartsaping using Aquaponics Water

Irrigation can be a very simple approach to expand the main benefit of one's aquaponics lawn to dirt plants, however, that you never want to utilize irrigation and hose irrigation methods with your water. These standard methods allow the majority of the water to evaporate or float away until the plant advantages of the moisture.

Smartsaping or even Xeriscaping usually identify wet landscaping, even at which the water necessary for desert plants has been delivered directly into the plant origin through small irrigation tubes. However, smartsaping methods may be utilized at a moist climate to deliver potable water directly into the roots of your plants.

The 3 main components of a smart scale backyard would be as follows:

- Hybrid Utilizing irrigation tube to provide water into plant roots
- Within the roots using mulch to Decrease evaporation
- Amending soil with mulch and other substances to Increase moisture retention at the Main zone

Once you use aquaponic overflow water to irrigate those engineered ground gardens, then you can grow any plant that thrives in your climate.

- The Least You want to learn to construct local gardening guidance to intending your aquaponic garden. There is no need to reevaluate gardening intellect.
- Use nature to cultivate plants that will flourish on your current weather requirements.
- In addition to vegetables and fruits, you're able to create flowers, herbs, trees, and also drifting plants in an aquaponics garden.
- For all those plants which want the soil to flourish, you're able to water and simmer beds using water in the tank for your fish.

TIPS AND TRICKS OF AQUAPONIC CULTIVATION

Over the span of conducting our system we've tried several methods of plants. It's been interesting seeing the gaps in the time to harvest from every. We originally started by purchasing suspended begins and placing them at the media and float beds. Comparable to field creation there's a plateau in development from the time that the crops have been planted to if they creep up the expanding pace. This is actually the acclimating stage at which the starts are becoming used to this new climbing networking, water, nutrient option not to mention the surroundings itself. The suspended begins even with all the acclimatization phase grew to crop size in a shorter period than if necessary. The down side of this will be that the frozen starts are somewhat pricier then seeds.

We attempted germinating seed from the computer system. We used a single inch rock wool plugs from the media and float beds. Each wide variety of seed needed another germination speed but complete the germination has been powerful. We seeded two carrot types and ginger. From the float mattress rock wool was put in individual websites and seeded. The sites have been at harvest dimension, approximately one and a half square ft. each. Using this method, the harvest was launched and chosen from precisely the exact same website. This did not provide us the option to begin at a nursery and boost the spacing by simply transferring the seedlings to the end sites as soon as they climbed to a particular size. At a trial setting that this works out completely but when we had been pushing the manufacturing efficiency we'd have missed that the two or three weeks we might have completed a harvest and began another in exactly the exact same moment.

Since the trial of seeding right into the float mattress was completing we started germinating from the press mattress in a few ways. We put a rock wool slab of sticks even using all the press level to guarantee enough moisture was evil up and seeded sufficient to populate the float mattress. This was done as a way to find that the germination achievement in the press bed and also to reduce the total amount of time that the crops were at the ending spacing of their float bed. As stated previously we could develop one harvest and begin another in precisely the exact same method, speeding up the crop time from harvest to harvest by a few weeks.

We also ventured into the press bed simply by putting the seed from the enlarged clay. Germination was powerful however, spacing became a problem. Control where every seed was put was tough and thickness of seeding was arbitrary at best. The seed transferred from side to side and also finished up in various depths because the seeds have been put and fall via the media. Additionally, since the seeds grew in the press they had been abandoned in position by seeding to harvest. For the faster crops such as lettuce the manufacturing time in complete spacing might have been cut in case began nearer together or at rock wool. For plants such as tomatoes this is not as a problem because the harvest proceeds to create past the very first crop.

As a portion of pure experimentation we chose cuttings out of a few geranium plants, set them into rock wool cubes and implanted them at the press bed. No misting was completed and the only water that they received was out of the ebb and flow of the press mattress in the computer system. Rooting occurred over a couple of weeks and fresh leaves came out. The same as rooting cuttings in normal greenhouse press the geraniums flowered until they'd happen if started from seed. The cuttings were in an adult condition and did not need to experience the juvenile period for a seedling would need. The geraniums performed really nicely.

Plants: could be inserted into the machine following the fish have been inserted along with the germs are processing their own waste to nitrates. At this stage nourishment are present and accessible to the crops. Within our aquaponics program we record out several kinds of plants best match for growing from the media and float beds. These plants vary from herbs and leafy greens.

Guru Hint: Experiment, play and have fun discovering the various approaches it is possible to utilize aquaponics, but monitor everything. Review the information and improve what possible. Grow -- Iterate -- Growth

Chapter 6
Microgreens

Microgreens for Commercial Grower:

Growing microgreens is a method for extending the extent of your activity to incorporate this to a great extent undiscovered market. We have never demonstrated our greens to a culinary expert who wasn't amped up for utilizing them. This energy is shifting into the customer showcase too, making request considerably more grounded. As an ever-increasing number of individuals are encountering the subjective contrast of crisp neighbourhood produce, your microgreens will sell without any problem. Offering your locale this all year asset can be an incredible method to enhance your activity. Another advantage these greens offer is their capacity to get speedy ranch salary while likewise adding to its ripeness.

On numerous farms it frequently takes at any rate several months to begin recovering the cash put resources into fertilized soils and manures. While the little ranch's essential spotlight isn't as a rule on making a buck yet rather the soundness of the land and its encompassing network, consistent salary is fundamental to addressing the necessities of the homestead and ranch family.

Microgreens require negligible starting venture, with most assortments costing under two dollars for every plate for seed and soil. When planted, they can begin creating pay in only a little while.

After your plate have been gathered, fertilizing the soil your dirt presently loaded up with stem and root matter is likewise fast and simple. In the warmth of the mid-year this dirt can be revised, treated the soil, and prepared to use in less than a month. We have made an uncommon worm container for this reason. As our plate are treated the soil, a lot of worm castings are added to the dirt, advancing it much further. Now it very well may be utilized to begin your seedlings, consolidated into your fields, or even used to develop more microgreens. With the entirety of their favourable circumstances, you can perceive any reason why microgreens can upgrade the little ranch.

For Home Grower:

Adjacent to their extraordinary taste and classy interest, microgreens are also unimaginably nutritious. The ability to accumulate and eat them inside minutes gives you access to their most restoratively rich state. They give us a strong bit of palatable supplements, minerals, and phytonutrients. While your taste buds benefit as much as possible from their extraordinary flavour, your body will get the compensations of their concentrated enhancements.

It's a remarkable thing to eat something so incredible that you get goose bumps from how brilliant and alive it is. We have been growing and eating microgreen plates of blended greens for a significant long time and still the general thought of fixing one for ourselves puts favours our faces. We are continually astounded at the sum we can eat at once; it's like drinking an infection glass of water on a rankling summer's day. Your body is in completed simultaneousness with your cerebrum that this, right now, is essentially the best thing you could give.

Children and Microgreens:

Growing microgreens isn't only for grown-ups! It tends to be an enjoyment and simple path for kids to interface with nature. Microgreens give a connecting with venture at home or at school, instructing about where nourishment originates from and how to develop it. Youngsters have all the more an association with things on the off chance that they are a piece of the procedure. Seeds become their seeds that develop into their greens. A personality and association are shaped with the plants and their advancement. Molly Kaizen portrayed this marvel when she discussed taking a gathering of school children to "The Pizza Farm" in northern California. The children invested energy watching and finding out pretty much the entirety of the segments that made up pizza; the cows that created the milk that made the cheddar, the fields that developed the wheat that they ground into flour to make the outside layer, and the growing herbs and tomatoes that made up the sauce. At that point, they made their own pizza. She portrayed the expectation as they trusted that their pizza will wrap up; every one checking each couple of minutes to check whether their magnum opuses were finished. This fervour doesn't occur while our little one's trust that solidified pizza will show up on their plates. It is a blessing to give our kids a consciousness of their nourishment and its procedure. Particularly in rural and urban regions, numerous youngsters today aren't exactly certain where nourishment originates from. In the event that one has never observed a carrot collected out of the earth, how might you realize that is the place it originated from? It could be similarly as intelligent that a carrot originates from a can or basically from the store. Beginning microgreens with your kids allows them to get their hands in the earth. It offers them the chance to find what else is growing in the dirt. It gets alive in their brains, as they watch worms separate their kitchen scraps or seeds spring to life. You may even locate your critical eaters requesting more greens on their supper plates! When this living world has been proposed, the conceivable outcomes are unfathomable. From a couple of straightforward seeds come fresh out of the box new eyes for nature.

Microgreens vs. Sprouts vs. Baby Greens:

Sprouts, microgreens, and child greens are on the whole stages in a plant's advancement. Every ha distinguishing attributes and fluctuating dietary benefits. A grow is the primary phase of a seed's advancement. "Sprout" is really synonymous with germination. Developed in various sorts of compartments, these seeds are kept soggy and at room temperature until they sprout. Rather than permitting them to develop in a medium and set up into a plant, grows are expended directly after they sprout. Regularly somewhat obscure and yielding a crunchy surface, they have gotten progressively famous for their healthy benefit.

At the point when developed in a medium (soil or something else), the second phase of a seed's advancement includes the foundation of its underlying foundations and the opening of its first leaves, called cotyledons. Greens reaped at this stage are called microgreens. On the off chance that microgreens are permitted to keep on growing, they put on their next arrangement of leaves, called "genuine leaves." True leaves are the leaves of a plant that recognize it from another plant. While numerous brassicas (cabbage, broccoli, arugula, and so on.) all have fundamentally the same as heart-formed cotyledons, when their actual leaves create, they look very changed and are handily recognized from one another. These greens are collected in their early stages, and are just permitted to develop in the dirt for up to 14 days. They have the entirety of the medical advantages of sprouts with the additional bit of leeway of follow minerals raised from the dirt they are developed in. At this stage their surface, appearance, and flavour are significantly more like a plate of mixed greens green than a crunchy grow. In the event that the seed were permitted to keep on growing past the genuine leaf stage and, given enough reality, it would inevitably arrive at the infant green stage. Child greens are delicate leaves that are well known in plate of mixed greens blends frequently called mesclun or spring blend. They are tastier and more delicate than leaves from a full-developed head of lettuce however lose a portion of the power of flavour and healthy benefit that they had at the microgreen organize.

Health and Microgreens:

As individuals, our fundamental establishments lie in the soil. But countless us have disregarded this noteworthy association over the span of the last barely any ages, our relationship with nature is so out of date and fundamental that it can't be completely excused. In case while we are eating, we take a short relief, we can without quite a bit of a stretch follow our sustenance back to the plants, the animals, the soil, and even the breeze, deluge, and sun. These things have their combination on the property. There is no avoiding that the adequacy of the earth and the prosperity of people are by and by tied.

Standard agriculture has been practiced for an enormous number of years wherever all through the world. Little extension and worked by hand, these farms are significantly widened and capably tended. Widened farmers make the craft of soil stewardship their basic work, developing in a way that truly adds to and improves the life of the estate and everything and everyone that interfaces with it. The animals raised here are alert with strong coats. The earth is rich, diminish, and sweet smelling. The plants are rich and grow vivaciously with negligible sign of pressure. The sustenance become here contributes evening out and prosperity to its incorporating system. To be sure, even the typical onlooker can see that "baffling something" that overruns the air around such a farm.

The greater a residence is in scale and the greater its mechanical objectives, the further it meanders from this separated little farm model. All through the main residual century there has been a persistent move in the scale and point of convergence of the farm at this moment. Prior to the completion of World War II, it was regularly envisioned that bleeding edge, mechanized mechanical structures were better than little extension customary methodologies. Close by industrialization came the beginning of substance fertilizer use in cultivating. After the war, an impressive parcel of the heightens that were used in the formation of bombs were changed into plant manures.

During this time, conviction that farms ought to have been gigantic to misuse the modern office hypothesis got hold. Various farmers got off the land and into the urban networks to join the growing example of industry. The family farm steadily evaporated as huge agri-business got hold.

Throughout the main outstanding century, the United States has lost over 4.5 million farms. As demonstrated by the U.S. specification office, the degree of people living and tackling farms has gone from 40 percent to under 1 percent. Close by this revamping of our nation's farms came the unpreventable exchange off of the idea of produce available. In Paul Bergner's book, The Healing Power of Minerals, Special Nutrients and Trace Elements, USDA estimations are consolidated that speak to this lessening. These figures show mineral and supplement substance declining in a couple of sorts of results of the dirt between the years 1962 and 1992. Among others, calcium dropped by pretty much 30 percent, iron by 32 percent, and magnesium by 21 percent. Produce sustenance is compelled by the idea of soil it was created, by the way it was procured, its treatment after gather, and how old it is once it shows up at your fork. To get a sentiment of how nutritious microgreens are, we ought to at first look at how these components impact the healthy substance of our produce.

Health and Soil:
The collaborations among plants and soil are so immense and complex that a few people have devoted their whole lives to contemplate them. From these

investigations, researchers are reaffirming what the conventional rancher has known for a large number of years; assorted variety is one of the keys to sound soil and thusly solid plants and animals. Yield turns, manures, soil corrections, supportable creature cultivation, and the growing of a wide assortment of vegetables all join into the extending decent variety and ripeness of the land. Produce developed in prolific ground can get a bounty of phytonutrients, minerals, and follow components. An attention on the strength of soil science prompts natural vermin and dry season obstruction, making a ranch that can support life inconclusively.

In ordinary horticulture, soil has become only a medium that holds our vegetables upstanding rather than the living, powerful power that it ought to be. Right now, soil the executives is viewed as in-effective and second rate. Centre, rather, is put for huge scope single-crop creation (mono-culture) and expansive range compound treatment. Within this framework, the tremendous measure of soil-improving systems is overlooked and supplanted with persistent uses of three water-dissolvable composts: nitrogen, phosphorus, and potassium (N-P-K). Natural life in the dirt is incredibly diminished, bargaining its wellbeing and respectability.

When this issue has started underneath the surface, indications start to emerge in the plant bodies. Out of nowhere the plant's characteristic protection from bugs, parasite, and ailment has been undermined, leaving it open and defenceless against assault. This issue is treated in ordinary agribusiness with the use of a wide scope of pesticides and fungicides. The outcomes appear to be successful. Less bugs, less illness, less generally speaking harm to the plant. To the unaided eye, the dirt despite everything looks dark coloured and the plant despite everything looks green. It appears to be a proficient, viable technique for controlling these undesirable factors.

Tragically, as the dirt keeps on being disregarded, vegetables are given heavier and heavier uses of these poisonous substances. In the end the synthetic concoctions must be unsafe to the point that unique suits and veils should be utilized to apply them. Now, if you somehow happened to investigate the surface, you would see the loss of organic life and the possible passing of the dirt. When the entirety of the microbial life has been executed, no measure of nitrogen, phosphorus, or potassium can bring it back. Soil that was once rich and fruitful gets inadmissible for farming. The dirt has become something to treat as opposed to something to construct and reinforce. This is reflected in the manner that cutting-edge medication thinks about the human body. Much time is spent tending to a patient's manifestations instead of taking a gander at the reason. As infections are getting more grounded, so are bugs. We continue expanding the measurements just to find that the foundation of the issue despite everything exists and the indications are getting increasingly hard to treat. Some have discovered an increasingly all-encompassing methodology—taking a gander at the entire body, the entire ranch, the entire earth—to be the answer for both human wellbeing and agribusiness. It is getting increasingly more of a standard thought that sound nourishment and a functioning way of life help with the life span and soundness of people.

Health and Harvesting:

The joint efforts among plants and soil are so monstrous and complex that a couple of individuals have dedicated their entire lives to mull over them. From these examinations, scientists are reaffirming what the customary farmer has known for countless years; grouped assortment is one of the keys to sound soil and in this manner strong plants and animals. Yield turns, composts, soil remedies, supportable animal development, and the growing of a wide collection of vegetables all join into the broadening not too bad assortment and readiness of the land. Produce created in productive ground can get an abundance of phytonutrients, minerals, and follow segments. A consideration on the quality of soil science prompts regular vermin and dry season hindrance, making a farm that can bolster life uncertainly.

In conventional cultivation, soil has become just a medium that holds our vegetables upstanding instead of the living, amazing force that it should be. At the present time, soil the administrators is seen as in-viable and below average. Focus, rather, is put for gigantic extension single-crop creation (mono-culture) and far reaching range compound treatment. Inside this structure, the huge proportion of soil-improving frameworks are neglected and displaced with diligent employments of three water-dissolvable manures: nitrogen, phosphorus, and potassium (N-P-K). Common life in the soil is unimaginably reduced, bartering its prosperity and decency.

At the point when this issue has begun underneath the surface, signs begin to develop in the plant bodies. Out of the blue the plant's trademark assurance from bugs, parasite, and affliction has been undermined, leaving it open and vulnerable against ambush. This issue is treated in common agribusiness with the utilization of a wide extent of pesticides and fungicides. The results seem, by all accounts, to be effective. Less bugs, less sickness, less as a rule mischief to the plant. To the independent eye, the earth notwithstanding everything looks dull shaded and the plant regardless of everything looks green. It gives off an impression of being a capable, feasible procedure for controlling these unfortunate components.

Shockingly, as the earth continues being ignored, vegetables are given heavier and heavier employments of these harmful substances. At last the engineered creations must be dangerous to the point that special suits and shroud ought to be used to apply them. Presently, on the off chance that you some way or another happened to research the surface, you would see the loss of natural life and the conceivable going of the soil. At the point when the total of the microbial life has been executed, no proportion of nitrogen, phosphorus, or potassium can bring it back. Soil that was once rich and productive gets forbidden for cultivating. The soil has become something to treat instead of something to build and strengthen. This is reflected in the way that bleeding edge prescription contemplates the human body. Much time is burned through watching out for a patient's signs as opposed to looking at the explanation. As contaminations are getting more grounded, so are bugs. We keep extending the estimations just to find that the establishment of the issue regardless of everything exists and the signs are getting progressively difficult to treat. Some have found an undeniably widely inclusive system—looking at the whole body, the whole farm, the whole earth—to be the response for both human prosperity and agribusiness. It is getting progressively to a greater degree a standard idea that sound sustenance and a working lifestyle help with the life expectancy and adequacy of individuals.

Nutritional Independence and Microgreens:

The joint endeavours among plants and soil are so colossal and complex that two or three people have committed their whole lives to think about them. From these assessments, researchers are reaffirming what the standard rancher has known for innumerable years; gathered variety is one of the keys to sound soil and right now plants and animals. Yield turns, fertilizers, soil cures, supportable creature advancement, and the growing of a wide assortment of vegetables all join into the widening not all that awful combination and preparation of the land. Produce made in gainful ground can get a plenitude of phytonutrients, minerals, and follow fragments. A thought on the nature of soil science prompts standard vermin and dry season impediment, making a ranch that can reinforce life uncertainly.

In traditional development, soil has become only a medium that holds our vegetables upstanding rather than the living, astonishing power that it ought to be. Right now, soil the overseers is viewed as in-reasonable and beneath normal. Centre, rather, is put for monstrous expansion single-crop creation (mono-culture) and broad range compound treatment. Inside this structure, the immense extent of soil-improving systems is dismissed and dislodged with persevering occupations of three water-dissolvable excrements: nitrogen, phosphorus, and potassium (N-P-K). Normal life in the dirt is incredibly decreased, bargaining its success and conventionality.

Right when this issue has started underneath the surface, signs start to create in the plant bodies. Out of nowhere the plant's trademark confirmation from bugs, parasite, and torment has been undermined, leaving it open and powerless against trap. This issue is treated in like manner agribusiness with the use of a wide degree of pesticides and fungicides. The outcomes appear, apparently, to be successful. Less bugs, less affliction, less generally speaking insidiousness to the plant. To the autonomous eye, the earth despite everything looks dull concealed and the plant paying little mind to everything looks green. It radiates an impression of being an able, doable strategy for controlling these heartbreaking parts.

Incredibly, as the earth keeps being overlooked, vegetables are given heavier and heavier vocations of these destructive substances. Finally, the designed manifestations must be risky to the point that exceptional suits and cover should be utilized to apply them. By and by, if you somehow happened to inquire about the surface, you would see the loss of common life and the possible going of the dirt. Right when the aggregate of the microbial life has been executed, no extent of nitrogen, phosphorus, or potassium can bring it back. Soil that was once rich and gainful gets prohibited for developing. The dirt has become something to treat as opposed to something to manufacture and reinforce. This is reflected in the manner that front line solution thinks about the human body. Much time is consumed keeping an eye out for a patient's signs rather than taking a gander at the clarification. As pollutions are getting more grounded, so are bugs. We continue stretching out the estimations just to find that the foundation of the issue paying little mind to everything exists and the signs are getting dynamically hard to treat. Some have discovered an evidently broadly comprehensive framework taking a gander at the entire body, the entire ranch, the entire earth to be the reaction for both human thriving and agribusiness. It is getting continuously to a more prominent degree a standard thought that sound sustenance and a working way of life help with the future and sufficiency of people.

Cruciferous Vegetables and Cancer Prevention:

There have been innumerable examinations done demonstrating the connection between malignancy counteraction and the utilization of cruciferous vegetables (i.e., all brassicas: broccoli, cabbage, arugula, and so on.). The crystalline mixes (indoles) found in cruciferous vegetables have a scope of medical advantages. Studies have indicated a huge decrease of instances of lung, bosom, colon, ovarian, and bladder malignant growth in individuals who eat an eating routine high in these vegetables. They contain an estrogen stabilizer, diindolylmethane (DIM), which is significant for the two people. The parity that this compound makes brings about more noteworthy protection from malignant growth just as the consolation of generally hormone balance. Malignancy development can be prodded by certain estrogen metabolites dynamic in the body. Diminish goes about as a deactivator, halting development. There has likewise been broad research done on the impacts of the phytonutrient sulforaphane, which is additionally inexhaustible in cruciferous vegetables. This amazing phytonutrient helps in detoxification, kicking off the liver's common inclination to flush the framework. Lamentably, it is difficult to expend the amounts of cruciferous vegetables expected to receive the rewards. Enter microgreens. Studies have indicated that one-and-a-half cups of full-developed broccoli has a similar measure of this phytonutrient as only one ounce of broccoli four days after it has sprouted. It is accepted that the youthful broccoli has twenty to fifty-fold the amount of sulforaphane as the completely developed.

Chapter 7
Pea Shoots, Sunflower Shoots, and Popcorn Shoots

Sometime around the middle of February, it seems to hit the weariness of satisfying my shopping basket using fresh veggies from California, Chile, Mexico, as well as Peru or New Zealand. No crime to the rocky farmers across the U.S. and around the Earth, since I genuinely appreciate the chance to eat apples through a snowstorm. However, these products need, by requirement, prolonged shipping times that sap them of taste and nourishment to a level. Nonetheless, it is not simple to consume local once you reside in a spot that needs budgeting 20 minutes each morning to scraping the ice from the windshield. The only way it could be completed in a little way is to grow that which you could inside, or tap to anything canning and dehydrating you achieved the summertime.

Because we are inclined to run from our food preservation concessions by March at our residence, we prompted us to start experimenting with easy-to-grow options, which led right into shoots.

Unlike Illness --that are increased in water and need meticulous scheduling for rinsing and maintenance to steer clear of bacterial problems --fires have been grown in the dirt; therefore, it is a cinch to become flexible concerning time, resource use, distance, and other significant facets. We started growing them only to find out what could happen, and our small farm is turning into a provider of shoots local restaurants--among them has dubbed a pea-shoot-laden veggie dish that the "Bossy Burger." Who would not wish to eat this? Likely, you will not start growing shoots such a vast scale, which you need to offer them from the pound to nearby eateries, but something is addicting about watching those shoots appear so fast.

The pea shoots possess a soul-quenching pinch and a delicate taste that tastes like spring up, anytime. Sunflower shoots are succulent, with a feel that is surprisingly firm also holds up nicely in a sauté. Popcorn shoots our main experiment whatsoever, is superbly peculiar in their own best. They seem somewhat like wheatgrass, however, flavor like quite youthful candy corn, then strike one with the aftertaste of corn stalk. I tend to combine all of the shoots to bargain with that amazing aftertaste, but a few folks have told me that they currently crave that taste. With these three options, shoots will be just a couple weeks away from flourishing under your lights, so let us begin.

Excellent Options for Growing Shoots

Overall, shoots are just microgreens of those seeds you have selected. Consequently, if you should allow the peas, sunflowers, and peppermint to develop into full adulthood, you would have those crops. But since you harvest them at this young age, the flavors are more extreme, and you'll be able to plant them closer together in a set tray.   Together with shoots, assortment does not often matter very far, but I have found better outcomes with a particular sort of pea seed. Here are some options:

- Dwarf Grey Sugar' peas: Following far experimentation, we currently utilize just those, possibly for our plantation and also for home growing. They are designed to be briefer peas, so if you would like to place a few in your backyard, it is possible to purchase pea pods without needing to perform trellising. For indoor climbing, I enjoy them since they're refreshing, easy to develop, and flavor surprising once you flip them into pesto. Virtually any pea seed could be turned in to shoots, but so if you have any 'Sugar Snap' pea seed in your home, which will get the job done. I would avoid varieties created to be stable and tall, however, like 'Oregon Giant.'

- Sunflower: Though I have got a listing of sources at the close of the novel, I had intended to steer clear of mention of particular seed firms in the principal body of this book because I do not wish to appear biased. But here I will violate my rule since there isone company that offers exceptional sunflower seeds such as shoots, plus they are organic. Johnny's Selected Seeds, a firm from Maine that offers a pumpkin seed collection that is highly count - capable and very hearty. While I've tried other options, it has been disappointing, mainly if I have played about with growing out of sunflower seeds, which are usually intended for bird claws (I said gardening is an experience, right?). Stick with seeds intended for human consumption, also provide Johnny's an attempt.

- Popcorn: On a whim, we believed whether we could purchase organic popcorn in the co-op, sprout this, then plant it and then consume it shoots. As it happens, the solution is yes. Thus, you do not have to purchase "seed" from anywhere so long as you've got access to soda - corn kernels that are not processed, either coated in acrylic or salted at all. Popcorn is different from corn kernels since popcorn comes from particular strains of corn, which were cultivated with the intention. It means that you may have the ability to sprout corn and receive precisely the same effect. However, popcorn is much more reliable if you are attempting to develop shoots.

- Nasturtium: Among of the most common edible blossoms, nasturtiums make delicious shoots. As when placing in the backyard, nasturtiums could be somewhat slow to the fold. Consider soaking the seeds in warm water for one hour or more before dispersing them at the press.

Trays, Pots, and Other Containers

Much as with other kinds of microgreens, I tend to favor open-style seedling trays using nominal thickness and drainage slots at the base. The slots maintain the dirt from amassing an excessive amount of moisture, which may quickly cause mold within a shoots tray, despite adequate ventilation.

That is because the seeds have been sown so near each other, which with irrigation, root rot could develop into a problem within only twenty-five hours of planting. When selecting a pot or tray, maintain dirt use in mind. Due to these origins, the shoots do not require the sort of soil thickness you would notice with plant begins or indoor herb gardens. Conserve dirt by Selecting a bigger container, also make crop simpler with a pot or tray that is shallow instead of deeper. Though peas, sunflowers, and corn demand lots of distance in regards to root thickness, when implanted as shoots, even a challenging thing occurs: the origins start to curl into one another, developing a thick mat in the instance of pea shoots, also turning your plate to a good cube. I tend to utilize shallow trays only because of this, since weathered the dirt after the crop is readily achieved, such as throwing a tiny rug on the mulch pile. Bonus for homesteaders: cows adore the leftover stalks and seeds from holes. Therefore, you use minimum dirt, get maximum usage from the plate, and possibly even create your cows contented.

Prep perform

For passions, I discover a pure mulch combination will work nicely, so long as it is instead "fluffy" in a sense.

If all you've got is indoor potting soil, then lighten this up by incorporating vermiculite into the ground. The absolute most significant part of soil prep would be to bring some water into the mixture before planting, which helps to maintain moisture during the germination stage.

When mixing fertilizer and water, go to get a consistency that is just like a crumbly brownie combination --then get a few and squeeze. If a couple of drops of water come out, then that is perfect. When there's a continuous flow of water, then it means you have made the mix too moist, and you ought to add more dry mixture. It is not compulsory to premoisten the dirt in this manner, and I have put a lot of trays which did well without it; however, I have discovered it may accelerate germination time with a couple of days in case you use this technique. For seed preparation, there is a straightforward approach to accelerate the germination period: simply boil the seeds for approximately twenty-four hours before planting. Sometimes, particularly when the home feels over the colder side, that I yank them for a day or two more, so they start to sprout until I plant them. This can decrease germination up to a week in some instances.

However, be very careful about massaging during warm weather and for a lot longer than a lot of daylight hours because after they pass on the point where they are sprouting, they will begin to deteriorate and cannot be implanted. The worst aspect of needing to plant or placing it off for a long time would be the fact that rotting, moist shoots seeds give off a stench that can permeate the home. Seriously, it is among the worst stinks you could picture, such as fungus-crusted toe jam interior wet, filthy socks. Simply make it a point not to learn if I am characterizing that odor accurately.

Planting and Care First measures

Be sure that you begin with a fresh tray, grass, or alternative container, and include only a couple of inches of the soil mixture, ensuring to "up against it" if needed. Since the mixture is moist, there is often a desire to push down the soil, but that produces a compaction problem that may turn your shoots into a hardened brick if it is placed under mild. Another factor when dispersing soil would be to have a little time to make a flat surface, particularly over the sides.

Regrettably, it's easy to Allow the dirt build up on both sides somewhat and return to some depression in the center; however, this accidental valley-like tray may lead to unevenness on your water supply, allowing a few seeds to sit down for a long time some dry outside. As soon as your soil mix is prepared, seed liberally. For shoots, which indicates you're going to be developing a seedbed in which the seeds seem too near together, but are not overlapping.

There is no need to poke holes in the dirt mixture and put seeds indoors, and they could sit together with the ground and develop perfectly well that manner. Bear in mind that every seed will develop a fire vertically; therefore, it is okay if they are all only a few fractions of an inch from one another, but you do not need them competing to get the specific same miniature stretch of dirt. Should you happen to sow them thicker and they are touching another in components, that is fine also, just understand that you may get less germination than ever anticipated.

The fantastic thing is these non-germinating seeds tend to find another chance after your first crop. Water quite lightly, then place a vacant black arrow on top of this micro arrow. This can help to keep the soil warm, also obstructing the light for a couple of days assists the seeds to become healthier generally.

You can glimpse indoors if you would like to observe the magical, but make sure you replace the cover when the seeds have not sprouted yet. As soon as they show any indication of expansion (approximately a few times), remove the water and cover every day. Put under lighting for eight hours daily. You're able to provide them a mix of natural light and sun if you are at a season or even a geographical area in which sunlight is sufficiently robust, but remember that the snaps will bend toward the light, therefore rotate the menu every day if needed. Otherwise, set the menu directly beneath your developing lights, approximately 6 inches in the tops of these plants.

Maintaining Growing

After they have established, shoots do not need much maintenance, and it can be a plus. But similar to microgreens, they profit considerably in the" floor watering" plan. Just fill out a kitchen sink, tub, another empty tray, together with approximately an inch of water, and also place the shoots into it for a couple of minutes. The plant will assume the water that it requires and moisturize the roots which way. This strategy is also helpful if shoots are appearing droopy and will need to replenish up.

In case you don't have a means to underside water, then water at the root level, or mist significantly rather than water. Shoots are just four season Plants (However, some period are far better than additional) if it is especially humid at home (summer in many instances) contemplate planting and replanting shoots just following the weather has cooled off. At Orientation River, we have attempted to develop shoots yearlong, and I have tried the same strategy in your home. However, there are unquestionably far better seasons than others concerningproductive growth.

Spring and autumn are perfect. With heat pads, winter brings slower expansion but plenty of shoots. Summertime, however, is barbarous for shoots in a home with central ac. If you don't adore playing with tweaking components continuously --warmth, more mowing, less mowing, underside watering, misting, much more airflow, more distinct positioning, etc.--I would suggest saving start growing for much more temperate seasons instead of summer.

Strategies for developing shoots

hereare various additional tactics for maintaining your shoots track :

- keep watering and supplying light into the shoots menu following a very first crop. Many instances, a few seeds germinate afterward or are postponed since they are under new seeds. For pea shoots, particularly, you can have two to three additional harvests due to this. These following harvests will not be as plentiful as the very first ones, but they are enough to be well worth the attempt.
- In the event the atmosphere in your home appears mainly dry, mist the plants whenever they are in a young phase of expansion and then place a crystal clear tray at the top. These can be found at any garden shop, plus they help to allow in light but
- Lock moisture. I find those values in winter, mainly when the shoots are still merely from the germination point, but maybe not established sufficient yet. Alternately, it is also possible to use plastic wrap around, but just make individual the shoots are not increased enough to bump from the cap of the wrapping, which may slow down growth.
- Another fantastic tactic once the atmosphere is dry is to mist the plants more frequently throughout the day should they appear to be fighting. Be conscious that this technique can cause searing if the crops are near a natural light source, therefore increase the mild or reduce the crops by 6 inches and then mist greatly if that occurs.

Troubleshooting

Shoots Some typical issues and Possible solutions such as shoots:

No more Germination, even after a couple of Days

Shoots often germinate fast; therefore, this could be a significant matter. Above all, it is regarding the temperatures of the ground. Placing a cap within the tray will maintain the warmth and moisture indoors, but you want an excess boost, so look at placing the tray onto a heating mat that can be found at any garden shop. These rectangular mats increase the temperature slightly, just enough to allow the seeds to feel comfortable, but not sufficient to harm them to scorch your counter. It is possible to make it plugged into days if needed. When it's been a week, and you are not visiting germination, assess the grade of your soil combination, and see whether it is overly tender -- compaction will frequently stop the seeds from launching.

Moldy Clumps within a Tray

Moldy clumps may be a consequence of improper airflow, overwatering, or even too much humidity. Whether there are untouched shoots from the menu, lift that segment (throw the moldy part) and move into another tray, allowing the soil to dry out a bit before you water. Wait a few days before picking to determine if mold grows with this section too;

In case it will discard and begin. In the event, the issue will be a lot of moisture from the beginning, which may occur during warm months, sow the seeds to dry dirt rather than pre-wetting the dirt mix, and also do a thorough watering before covering the groove during the germination procedure.

Cases of those Shoots Are Browning or Turning Dark

You've got them too near the light source, and that means you are cooking them at the tray. Move them away from your mild by another 6 inches, then clip off the hints mentioned above, and the rest will flourish.

Shoots Are Yellowing or Seeking Droopy Normally, and yellowing means overwatering, therefore allow your soil dry out a bit. By comparison, droopy fires are frequently brought on by under watering, or from a lot of humidity. If that's the circumstance, bottom water that the shoots in cold water and see whether they perk up after roughly ten to fifteen minutes. Additionally, fix your buffs so that shoots are receiving some airflow to distribute stagnant, humid atmosphere and boost flow. Bear in mind that plants "breathe," and they want some warmth to maintain oxygen levels. If your attempts are not sufficient and the shoots continue being droopy, you might only need to harvest and consume --they will continue to be tasty and healthy, only a little less eloquent. Storage Factors Much like microgreens, shoots do most beautiful kept in glassand may last for weeks in the refrigerator in this manner. Pea shoots, even though fragile, are unusually long-lasting and maintain their crunch until the ending. Sunflower shoots are more stringent, and I have retained a few for three months in the refrigerator without

Any discernable shift in taste. Popcorn shoots, however, often last for some time and if retained for more, that strange aftertaste gets more powerful. So for all those, I might harvest and consume the identical moment.

Harvesting and Preservation

Getting Prepared to Choose for every Selection of shoots, There's a Perfect Time for the crop:

- Pea shoots these can develop long and seem unkind, and that I have a tendency to crop them if they are approximately 8 to 10 inches. If you'd like sweeter and much more uniform shoots, then harvest around 4 inches if they are just starting to unfurl their leaves. If you'd like a super-rich harvest, and also a pea-sweet flavor, then make them go till 12 inches. Longer than this, however, and they begin to get too heavy and long to get the tray, which means they begin flattening. Additionally, the taller they acquire, the further succulent the taste.

- Sunflower shoots these taste best once you buy them until the sunflowers create their first real leaves. In the shooting point, you will have two well crispy petals. If the first real leaves start tinkering, they develop involving those petals and possess a scratchy texture, which I do not like, although they're perfectly edible. Should you allow the shoots to opt for too long and the leaves begin coming up, then you are still able to delight in the shootsonly flavor and appear by plucking off the leaves that are true and shedding them. With regards to what to crop,

I clip all of the ways to the ground since the stalks are just as yummy as the leaves.

- Popcorn shoots. These are greatest at approximately 6 inches, and make sure you incorporate a number of those white-and-pink bottoms, in which the most extreme taste resides. When the shoots are becoming taller, they are fun to get from the windowsill only because they seem so lively, but the flavor grows increasingly more mountainous since they mature. At approximately ten inches, then the shoots have all of the taste and appeal of new lawn clippings.

Chapter 8
Herbs

Among the most gratifying jobs for almost any kitchen gardener is the herb kettle, brimming over with favorites such as sage or pops, or ripe using a medley of different mints. I have seen some Fantastic mixes collectively --such as making a "pasta sauce herb pot" with lavender, thyme, and basil--because most herbs flourish from average harvest, they are ideal for a kitchen area because that you can just snip precisely what you will need for a specific dish. For my kitchen area, I love to place blossoms in separate baskets so I can isolate them from the event of pest problems or mold issues. However, I frequently produce mixes when giving herb baskets like gifts, and I love the scents that combine as a consequence of enabling them to appear collectively.

Generally, many blossoms have been well-geared toward indoor climbing, and many of those anglers I understand report their outside garden blossoms since the weather gets sharp so that they can expand the growing season inside. Many herbs, like rosemary, rosemary, thyme, and lavender, spread well if you choose a cutting out of a present indoor or outdoor plant and then prepare it for expansion indoors. If that is your plan, just cut on a 4-inch segment (measured from the tip of the stem/ foliage below the ground) and strip away about an inch or so of their reduced leaves. Set the stem to some potting mixture, like vermiculite, and maintain the mixture somewhat moist since the plant disappeared. These crops such as humidity, therefore, cover with transparent glass or plastic allowing light, however, trapping moisture but do not let them get too warm from sunlight. Additionally, eliminate their covers sometimes or set them onto a porch or "transitional" area to provide them some atmosphere. This technique works nicely for transplant bought at a greenhouse, which should be "hardened" to temperature variations.

In my experience, there are occasions when I simply cannot appear to grow particular herbaceous plants from seed (I am looking in the basil) and that I want the jumpstart a transplant could offer. As soon as I started my indoor climbing experiences, I depended on a transplant nearly entirely since I appreciated having the ability to bypass that first significant jump in germination. Nowadays, but I delight in the planting procedure, and tend to select herbs that flourish best in my kitchen. Therefore, for this particular section, we will have a better look at just how to select from seed to crop, and that means that you can find a sense of growing herbs entirely inside. Should you move the transplant or herb-cutting path, however, a lot of the data still applies, especially in regards to problems like soil temperatures and drainage.

Great Varieties for Indoor Growing

Though many herbs do attractively in an indoor expansion area, some forms can be unbelievably fickle if you are attempting to grow from seed. Here are some options, broken down by degree of difficulty:

Easy Like a Sunday Morning

- Peppermint and spearmint: Hearty and extensive, mint enjoys to invade the land of different crops, so as soon as you've obtained it, keep ahead of harvesting it. If You'd like a robust mint flavor without developing a Lot of it, then Elect for soda - mint, as It offers a more intense taste

- Lemongrass: You do not plant this one out of seed: simply purchase a stalk of lemongrass out of a grocery store or farmers' market, cut the shirt, and place the stem in a couple of inches of water. The stem will create roots by itself and heaps of fresh shoots, and you're able to harvest from them. ∫ Exotic Steak: This number is known as more comfortable to develop than other types of hay. Also, it's as much taste.

- Additionally, it's quite significant and will last for weeks Requires Effort, but Ordinarily Doable

- Parsley: Normally rather simple to develop, but germination may be hit and miss. Typically, you are going to start to see expansion approximately two weeks following planting, and it tends to grow slower compared to other herbaceous plants generally.

- Oregano: The key using oregano is providing sufficient plant light daily; it might necessitate placing the marijuana beneath another bulb that is to get a couple of hours over the other blossoms. Typically, approximately eight hours of lighting is greatest ∫ Thyme: This herb also needs more mild, so that I frequently place rosemary and thyme in precisely the same area or put them alongside each other at a window.

- Rosemary: I have discovered my indoor rosemary stems from slough off rosemary in my backyard, but additionally, it is somewhat simple to grow from seed. Look out for more overwatering, because rosemary will favor drier dirt, and Make Sure You choose a selection that works well with indoor climbing, such as 'Blue Spire

- Chervil: Quite uncommon, but very flavorful, chervil is linked to parsley and contains a subtle taste. The herb does nicely in low-light places, which makes it an incredible selection for kitchen corners and out-of-the-way stains, but remember it does not work nicely when temperatures start to grow beyond 70 degrees, so judge your home's temp before planting.
- Cilantro: Here is another one that develops remarkably well outdoors but demands a higher degree of maintenance inside. To start with, it does not transplant well. Therefore it has to be made from seeds or starter plants. Also, it takes lots of drainages and nonetheless needs more nourishment, which makes it hard to maintain the dirt nourished. It will do good after it is established, however until then, intend on providing the herb fertilizer biweekly, which is twice as far as the other herbaceous plants. Additionally, water only when the soil appears quite dry.
- Basil: It is so omnipresent in cooking, so you would think basil is a cinch to grow in your garden. However, no. Notoriously tough to grow indoors from seed, basil will function best as a plant begins out of a greenhouse. Additionally, these lush Italian Steak leaves might not be wide and reasonably as you possibly find in a backyard. Somewhat I lean toward types with smaller leaves such as 'Dark Opal' or even Thai basil.
- Sage: " It is not too tough to acquire sage began inside, but it is likely to pass with overwatering. There have been a lot of instances where I visit those thick leaves and believe the plant appears dry, and then I wind up killing it as it's already nicely ventilated. Additionally, many experts suggest waiting a very long time before picking while the plant becomes established--around a year sometimes. For me, the area in my kitchen growing region is too confined to nurse a plant, which takes weeks before I could use it, but I do like to get a little pot moving since the herb dries well after crop.

Soil Prep

Herbs are somewhat finicky when it comes to drainage. Many gardener intellectsare they "do not like wet feet," meaning that when their roots become too rancid, rust can result. Every plant kind covered in this publication (except nausea) depends upon appropriate drainage to a level, however for blossoms, it is particularly crucial since they are inclined to enjoy a humid environment, which makes them vulnerable to root rot. Merely utilizing a pot with holes at the bottom is not sufficient, and if you purchase a typical kind of marijuana using a dish that grabs water, then you are going to be in even more trouble. This frequently contributes to a plant sitting water, which is practically always a terrible position for your plant. There are lots of approaches that could be useful for raising drainage. Some anglers use a method made for developing cactus since these specialty combinations are intended to drain fast, but I discover that just blending sand and vermiculite (at the ratio of a one-to-four component) collectively tends to make a joyful mix.

In case you are transplanting from outdoors, do as far as possible to eliminate the current garden soil by lightly shaking or tapping on the roots. You will not have the ability to remove all the dirt, but if it is possible to get most of it, then you will significantly lower your exposure to backyard insects and diseases. Anything you use, a fantastic strategy to reduce compaction, is to nurture inside the pot each month approximately. You can simply Have a fork and lightly loosen the dirt inside the container, taking care to remain mainly on the periphery so that you don't harm the roots.

Trays, Pots, and Other Containers

At the risk of harping a lot on drainage, and I'm likely to highlight the value of drainage.I will also place it in italics in case it helps: drainage. Herbs simply don't succeed at all in almost any circumstance where they are sitting, therefore select a pot or container which enables ample flow. You can indeed try out growing cilantro on your midst school lunchbox or skillet in that repurposed table or another remarkable container appeals to you personally, but if you would like to maintain the herbs heading to get a significant long time, then drill several holes and perhaps even throw a few pebbles at the ground. Your herbaceous plants will probably thank you. Beyond this, any substance functions; however, I tend to shy away from terra cotta pots since they create the blossoms dry out quicker, which melts my estimation of how much watering they require. Due to limited space, I apologize toward smaller containers, but in case the herbs start to spread a lot over the borders, or I wish to invite them to get larger, I will repot into a bigger container.

Planting and Care First Measures

Having the container and dirt blend prepared, and provide the mix a few glasses of water so that it's slightly moist. This helps your seeds from changing when you water them. Sow the seeds about a few times more durable than the magnitude of this seed.   That is a rule of thumb, and that which is generally meant for me is that if it is a teensy little seed, then I will barely push it in the ground, then I'll cover it with only a bit of vermiculite. When the seeds are more prominent, I would press half an inch and cover it. Water gently, then cover the container or pot with plastic kitchen

Wrapping. This is going to keep the soil seed and mix hot, to promote germination. Set the container or pot in a bright place or below a mild, and once the seedlings emerge, then remove the plastic wrap.

Maintaining Growing

Some herbs need specialized attention, but Generally Speaking, most may benefit from these suggestions for maintaining erections going strong:

- Fertilize every ten days or so with diluted fish mulch, located in any garden shop. At a pinch, I have also soaked rosemary in warm water for a couple of hours, allow it to cool, then sprayed that onto the crops. However, for this to be more "at a pinch" strategy, you would need to be among those Men and Women who appear to possess dried seaweed from the cabinet.
- Herbs such as humidity, but it is not always simple to tweak this illness, particularly in the summer months. One good strategy is to produce a tray of little stones or pebbles and then fill the tray with water, leaving approximately 1/4 inch of the best dry. Set the pots in addition to the trays making sure they do not touch the water, and the evaporation procedure will help to maintain the atmosphere at a beautiful humidity level.
- Give blossoms a routine "tub" by misting every couple of days. Does this help keep your hydrated, but also, it cuts down to pest issues because diminished plants are more susceptible to insects such as aphids and spider mites?
- Water at the bottom of this herb, not just leaves. This will enable the plant to become hydrated, without having it too "flattening out" from an excessive amount of water hitting on the leaves.

Troubleshooting

Herbaceous One of the common issues and Possible solutions for herbaceous plants:

Slow Growth or Limited Germination

Potentially, this might be a mild matter. Herbs need five or more hours of light each day to remain healthy, and full-size sunshine (given that the place is not overly hot) is best. However, in winter, even just a south-facing window may be inadequate. If you see slow growth, consider expanding the time in which the herbs are below mild up to two hours if needed.

Brown Patches or even Withered-Looking Candles When your herbs are beneath a light source, they could be too near the bulb. Mostly, you're burning.Herbs

Ought to be 6 to 8 inches from the light source, which space will be measured from the bulb into the peak of the plant.

Whitish Fuzz on Soil

This may be organic seed germination, but it might also be mold. Confirm that you are not overwatering--should you place your finger to the soil mixture and sense moisture instantly, then that may be the situation. Allow the plant "dry " and isolate it in the other crops in the meantime. Eliminate the moldy places, but bear in mind you might want to begin with this one.

Stems Seem Soft or Mushy

This could be an additional prevalence of overwatering. Stems often feel soft when root corrosion is happening. Another significant sign of issues is that a filthy odor mixed with all the beautiful herb aromas.

Bug Infestation at Progress

It is so disheartening to lean over a kettle of herbs, prepared to snip off a couple of choices for supper, and see something else is before you at the buffet.If it comes to pass, isolate the plant and then attempt a soap spray. This is a mixture of gentle liquid soap (such as Dr. Bronner's) along with also water. Spray in the day since the program once the plant remains in sunlight may cause bleeding.

Harvesting and Preservation

Getting prepared to decide on Each herb is chosen in its way, but generally speaking, go to the "old" leaves, which are complete. Start looking for new development, typically close to the middle of this plant, also prevent clipping near that region as you don't wish to shorten the life span of this herb. When your plant begins to blossom, snap the flowering area Once Possible to lengthen the plant's interval --such as many crops, herbs start flowering for a sign they're done growing (it is a procedure referred to as "bolting"). By taking away the flowers, you're able to fool the plant to sticking around for more essentially. When picking, remember that stalks often possess abundant flavor too. For example, cilantro stalks are equally as intensely flavored because of the leaves.

Storage Concerns

Because of a current homesteading kick, I have been experimenting with several strategies to conserve virtually everything, from roasted cabbage into dried celery.

In comparison to trying to conserve artichokes, blossoms are a breeze. There are many strategies to be confidentyour herbs may last for weeks. The fastest method is via drying--easily create a package, strip about an inch of leaves to expose just stalks, tie with twine or even a rubber ring, and hang in a cool, moist location. There is a part of my cellar which smells quite remarkable at this time, as a result of numerous capsule packages. The Benefit of drying will be that you can depart the packages hanging for very some time, or only crumble them whenever they are dehydrated and set them into jars. Another storage option would be preservation in olive oil. Be sure the glass jar is extremely dry, then fill it with herbs such as peppermint, thyme, and peppermint, in addition to some other ingredients such as garlic. Fill the jar with olive oil, making sure the oil fully covers the blossoms, also in approximately fourteen days, the petroleum is going to be infused with taste.

Following that, it is possible to strain the herbs and then drizzle the brand new generation over anything you enjoy. In the same way, you can finely chop herbs, set them in a glass jar, and cover entirely with honey. In fourteen days, the taste will infuse the honey, and in this scenario, I do not attempt to strain the herbs out. This mixture may be utilized instead of jam on toast, or even a few folks only eat a spoonful whenever they are feeling energy drained, mainly if more herbal herbs are traditionally utilized. In general, herbaceous plants are a leading addition to any kitchen garden, also integrating just a couple of favorites might help enhance the tastes of your meals. Now, I am irritatingly snobby in regards to "new" herbs whom I see in the supermarket because they seem so exhausted and exhausted. Knowing my herbs are chosen just about ten minutes until I love these makes me feel nostalgic, particularly in the winter, after this amount of freshness could be quite so tough to reach otherwise.

Chapter 9
Sprouts

When you are short on resources and space, sprouts create a simple indoor climbing endeavor. Essentially, you simply need seeds, a glass jar (more on this shortly), a few cheesecloths, or a thin dishtowel and sew! You are on your way into getting a sprout specialist. Nutritionally, sprouts can also be packed with fiber, enzymes, amino acids, vitamins, antioxidants, and other snacks, which help enhance your immune system and maintain your wellbeing on track. Additionally, they are delicious and rather straightforward to develop consistently. I tend to undertake a more rapid growing session at the depths of the winter, when other crops may be slowing within their progress. At a Minnesota February, even microgreens will take more time to turn out of seed to lush green carpeting. Therefore sprouts assist me in receiving a nutritional supplement while I am waiting.

Not all Sprouts allure to me personally in terms of flavor, however, and it is very likely you'll make the same discovery I enjoy sprouts using a kick like a peppermint or mustard, but people with a more earthy flavor (such as alfalfa) aren't my groove.   And that is okay since there are loads of options when it comes to selecting which kind of sprouts to increase, and discover everything you enjoy is a portion of this sprouting adventure.

Great Varieties for Indoor Growing

There are lots of options in regards to sprouting, and similar to microgreens, they encircle a substantial chunk of the vegetable kingdom. It's possible to sprout dill seeds, fenugreek, chives, legumes, wheat germ, and a lot of other people. Since you get more confident in your sprout installation, you can play with various options, and however, in terms of getting started, these are a few popular options:

- Alfalfa: This is the timeless sprout, using light and nutty flavor. Also, it creates a pleasant starting point for sprouting.
- Broccoli: Research at Johns Hopkins University reported that broccoli sprouts also pose an "exceptionally abundant supply of inducers of enzymes that protect against chemical compounds." Plus: yummy.

- Mung bean: lots of kinds of beans can be sprouted, and that is among the very jazzy. I am not fond of the flavor, but I have talked to folks who eat them daily and locate them creamy and yummy.
- Blends: If you shop on the internet for sprouts in places like Sprout-people.com, then you will come across quite a few combinations with some kinds of seeds, and it is almost always an excellent option. For example, an "Italian Combination" will couple clover, garlic, and cress, or even a grain mixture might consist of wheat, rye, oats, Kamut, and quinoa. These are typically an extremely cost-effective approach to buy multiple kinds of seeds without purchasing them separately.
- Others: In principle, you can sprout any seed that you desire. In practice, some only taste better compared to many others. Besides another sprout with this particular page, seed catalogs and merchants promote a number of these following: fenugreek, daikon radish, edamame legumes, spinach, sunflower, buckwheat, and onions.

Trays, Pots, and Other Containers

There are lots of options in regards to abundant sprout development, and take a look at the Resources page at the rear of the book for several excellent websites to search for supplies. If you anticipate developing sprouts frequently, look at obtaining a sprouter. These devices vary from a tiny, cup-like container that is generally around $10 into some multitray sprouted, which allows you to develop multiple kinds of sprouts concurrently. This bigger sprouter may be enjoyable, making little sprout skyscrapers on your kitchen, but remember you'll want to keep together with this procedure in case you've got multiple sprout kinds growing on various timeframes.

Sprouts are not hard to develop. However, they do need particular care completed at fixed intervals, and therefore unlike shoots or perhaps microgreens, you cannot begin them and go off for a couple of days. But if you are turning right into a sprout enthusiast along with your counter is consumed with too many containers and jars, a multitray sprouter might be precisely what you want. But if you are only getting started and you also wish to experiment using only one sprout variety at one moment, then reevaluate your installation by using just a glass jar (I use a quart-sized Mason or even Ball jar) plus a few cheesecloths or a thin dishtowel for putting over the surface. The sprouting seeds will probably require some airflow but will probably be allergic to dust, therefore refrain from having a milder lid because it can trap moisture.

Prep Work

First, ensure your jar or sprouter remains clean. And I am clean. Sprouts are already vulnerable to mold difficulties, and thus don't have an opportunity by believing a few dried flecks of meals or any dust will not be a significant thing. You do not have to bleach out the container but require a few minutes to test it thoroughly after washing and be sure it's prepared. When searching containers for sprouting, I favor hand-washing them to utilizing my dishwasher since I believe they make a much better scrub like that.

Planting and Care First Steps

Place about a tablespoon of seeds on your jar or container and cover them with

A couple of inches of hot water. I tend to work with filtered water because I find that I get much better results this way, but occasionally use tap water when I am in a hurry. Listed below are steps out of there:

- Permit the seeds to soak overnight, up to twenty-five hours if you are sprouting bigger seeds such as beans.
- In the morning, or after the boil, drain All the water, instead, although the cheesecloth, therefore, it acts as a filter.
- Fill the jar with a few more inches of clean water, and then drain through the filter.
- Put in place with indirect lighting.
- Place in water, and now set the jar back in your counter.
- Duplicate this procedure --drain, simmer to wash, drain, fill with water every morning and day (every twelve months, approximately) for the subsequent four to six weeks, before the sprouts have become a point where you are all set to crop them.
- Before ingestion, provide the sprouts last beverage, and get up to from these as possible. Then you can just set the jar in the fridge.

Troubleshooting

Some typical issues and potential remedies for nausea:

Flu Types from the Jar

Of all of the issues with sprouts, here can be the biggest. You truly have to remain on top of this rinsing program, since otherwise, you are going to get a mushy, moldy mess and might need to begin. If this comes to pass, throw the carrots out (even when they have got a tiny mold patch) and begin again, make sure you sterilize the jar until you do. If the issue keeps occurring, look at employing a separate container to the sprouting, like a sprouter or even a tray.

Sprouts Seem to Be Taking over Six Days

In case you are living in a chilly climate, then sprouts may take somewhat longer to reach adulthood. It's possible to accelerate the procedure by soaking the seeds overnight before putting them at a sprouter or jar. This will aid the seeds to germinate quicker. Additionally, you can decide on a sprouting type, which is going to be on a quicker schedule, such as beans. This class contains kidney beans, adzuki beans, cowpeas, garbanzos, and legumes. Beans frequently take just approximately two to four times from multiplying to adulthood.

Sprouts Are Increasing, but Do Not appear to Make "Greening Up."

Even though sprouts are useful within a place with indirect lighting, occasionally, they require an increase of photosynthesis. If your sprouts aren't getting green, then move the container into a place with more magnificent lighting, or near a window. Just be sure it is not in direct sun, because that may dry the carrots out. Additionally, remember that not all sprouts will be more green. For example, mung beans are a fairly, translucent white when fully sprouted, using a yellowed hint that results in the seed husk.

Harvesting and Preservation Getting prepared to Pick

If you "crop" sprouts, then it merely means that you pull them from their glass container and then consume them. What can be simpler? Just ensure they pass the smell test-- also when I have eaten out of a jar of sprouts, I will smell them before placing them in my salad. That is, as there are frequent warnings regarding sprouts being correlated with outbreaks of Salmonella and E. coli, that may take place if the sprouts have been permitted to sit for a long time. When that happens, bacteria may form, and also the tender sprouts are more vulnerable. I have discovered that smelling the carrots before eating averts problems. If they're off whatsoever, the odor is detectable, in my own experience. When in doubt, always throw it away.

Storage Concerns

Sprouts do not keep well, and also, if you place the jar from the fridge, the maximum shelf life you are likely to have would be about weekly. Then, that may be pushing it. The sprouts will start to demonstrate corrosion by getting somewhat mushy, and until long mold will shape. The best strategy with sprouts would be to eat them within a couple of days once they are fully grown.

Chapter 10
Mushrooms

Just a little Forest Right in Your Countertop

For me, mushrooms have just a small bit of puzzle. Perhaps it's because I grew up eating just the salty, salty mushrooms which came sliced, thrown into a pumpkin. The only new mushroom experiences I had as a child would be the occasional fleck at a can of cream of mushroom soup--and believe me, and if you reside in the Midwest, you are very likely to eat the fat in cream of mushroom soup, because it creates the base of roughly 75% of potluck dishes (the remainder is Jell-O). Thus, when I eventually ate "actual" mushrooms as an adult, this is a sin. Nowadays, I search out exotic mushrooms and Conquer men and women who forage to them. Additionally, once you're standing in the co-op and taking a look at the astronomical cost of morels, you most likely say, "Who'd pay that much for mushrooms" The solution is. It appears plausible that I would be eager to grow indoors, and I have made many efforts to maintain a vast selection of mushrooms, but tell the truth, there are just a few forms that do the job nicely (see the types section for more information) within my own space.

I have attempted to maintain logs grapple with shiitake spawn in my cellar, but it can be quite tricky to maintain humidity and humidity amounts ideal if you are attempting to grow out of logs inside. Let us have a few simpler avenues instead.

Get Prepared

Great Media for Indoor Growing When choosing which kind of mushroom that you would like to increase, it is crucial to choose spawn (that is what mushroom "newcomer" is known as) that functions nicely with whatever medium you have selected. For example, oyster mushrooms grow best in capsules, while wine caps succeed in sawdust. When making a decision, select your moderate first, then find out precisely what mushrooms grow nicely inside. Here's a quick cheat sheet:

Sawdust: The advantage of utilizing sawdust is it's cheap, and you will generally purchase tiny bags of it in a garden shop. Make sure you acquire the fine-grained sawdust instead of the substance that is nearer to woodchips. The mushrooms that perform well in this medium are all shiitake and wine limit.

Straw: Since it retains moisture but also allows for a beautiful quantity of warmth, straw is a beautiful medium for mushrooms, broccoli, and oyster mushrooms to develop exceptionally well in capsules. There are lots of sorts of straw. However, wheat germ will be very best for growing.

Hardwood block: A good option for first-time thieves is that a "table upper farm," that functions as a part of an abysmal log, or comprised within a wooden sawdust block. You merely should water, fix humidity levels as educated, and appreciate. These cubes have restricted fruiting occasions, unlike the number of that spawn increased in straw or sawdust, but they also generally have more exceptional success prices. You buy pre-inoculated logs for about $30-$40: those can yield a dozen approximately shiitakes everythree weeks when the fruiting starts. Or you can inoculate your log or logs using shiitake spawn.

One factor to remember when ordering is That Lots of mushroom spawn providers will only ship through specific days of the year. For example, leading provider Field & Forest may send mushroom kits just from November till May, though it does send certain kinds of spawn year-round. Moreover, make sure to buy spawn rather than spores. It is possible to utilize dyes (which are like seeds) for indoor climbing, instead of spawn, which will be similar to purchasing transplants with origins formed, but it requires quite a little expertise, patience, time to develop out of spores.

Prep Work

When you are using a straw for a mushroom moderate, here is where it is going to find a bit bizarre. Decrease the odds of disease difficulties, it is ideal for pasteurizing the straw, and therefore, you have to nourish it. I am not kidding. Set a large pot of water in the stove, allow it to boil for about twenty minutes as you're chopping down the straw to a manageable dimension, typically approximately 1 to 3 inches. I usually just grab a few straws, take it over a bowl and then cut it with scissors I purchase 2-inch strands. Many folks use a blender or food processor; however, I have discovered the cleanup with that process to be overly time-consuming.

Once the water has been boiling for some time, reduce the temperature to just beneath a boil, then also use a meat thermometer to check the water, which ought to be between 160 and 170 degrees Fahrenheit. After that, insert the straw into the water, and then induce any drifting straw (there'll be a lot) below the water using a skillet. Ideally, all of the straw should stay beneath the water, so if you can, burden the straw, which has a little grate, Pyrex dish, or even alternative heat-resistant product. Continue checking the warmth of this water to be sure it remains within reach and "cook" the straw for approximately 45 minutes. After that, switch off the cooker, allow the sew fresh for approximately ten minutes, then drain the water out of the kettle. Do not throw the water away. You can utilize it "straw juice" to your mushrooms after, providing them a nutrient kick.

Eliminate the straw out of the bud, allow it to come to room temperature before spawning. It will Start to dry; however, it is useful to possess the straw to be moist after presenting the spawn. You might even get a pasteurized straw, but where is the fun in that? In this manner, your kitchen may odor "army" to get no less than a day or two.

Planting and Care First Measures

Wash your hands along with the prep area thoroughly. Mushroom spawn is vulnerable to illness, and using a sterile environment is especially important. Shred your straw or evenly disperse your sawdust on your container, then mix in a few used coffee grounds. If you are a tea drinker, then it is worthwhile to pop up right into a nearby coffee shop and Request a small bucket of reasons --they generally throw them off anyway, and many stores close to urban gardening attempts are utilized to all those kind of orders.

The coffee grounds are packed with enzymes that supply a significant boost to a mushroom spawn, and besides, they help reduce the number of germs that may compete with your spawn. Your spawn will generally seem like a block of quite old cheese. Break this up in very tiny crumbles and incorporate it with all the straw or sawdust. Sometimes, the spawn will probably be from sawdust, and that means you merely need to add it into another, thicker coating of the substance. Concerning a container, then you may use many different containers, but among the most well-known approaches is to package a plastic bag using the moderate and spawn, then poke holes in it every 3 inches or so. This will permit airflow while keeping the entire package rancid and warm. Alternately, you can use a plate or baking pan and then spread the mix evenly, which Provides the mushrooms more space to grow. Distribute some potting soil on the surface, then mist completely. Set the pan or bag in a cool, dark place, including a cellar. You might even utilize a garage provided that the temperature is about 50 degrees Fahrenheit. Mist the mix periodically if it appears like it is beginning to become dry. You may start to observe a whitish fuzz grow --do not worry, it is not molded. For mushrooms, mold is probably to be black, yellow, pink, or bluish-green.

Troubleshooting

Some typical issues and potential remedies for mushrooms:

No First Growth Occurring

This could occur once an area is too trendy, or you do not have sufficient moisture. If you have been misting the mushrooms regularly, consider placing a germination mat below your container. In the event the challenge is moisture, then consider setting a moist towel above the container for a couple of days so that moisture could be included better. Do not leave it for a long time, however, because the mushrooms require a little fresh air to reduce carbon dioxide buildup.

Multiple Mushroom Growing Efforts:with no Results

Perhaps you have tried both straw and sawdust, you have altered your containers, attempted different rooms at home and corners of the cellar, possibly even sung into the spawn. And you're getting nothing. Sadly, this sometimes happens even with temperatures and moisture control. In cases like this, you might choose to put money into indoor gardener apparel. I guarantee this is not cheating. These kits are extremely well created for climbing and frequently assemble with mycologists (mushroom specialists) that are super informed about making options for indoor surroundings. Opt for a kit that is either one of those "tabletop plantation" types, or

Only an easy tote full of spawn and sawdust (occasionally with java thrown) that just has to be watered at regular intervals.

Harvesting and Preservation

Getting Ready to Harvest

Based on the number, mushrooms must be all set for a while at around three weeks. Typically, the best indication of adulthood is the caps will probably separate from the stalks. At that point, just select them.

Storage Concerns

Do not wash the mushrooms until you are prepared to prepare them for a meal; this can let them survive longer. Place them in a brown paper bag (not in plastic), and Shop in the refrigeratetor. A plastic container can trap moisture, whereas the newspaper bag absorbs any extra moisture coming from the mushrooms. Should you have to shop eggs for more, look at dehydrating them cook them, and freeze them.

Chapter 11
Lettuce

Radishes, Carrots, Tomatoes, and Other Compounds Many plants using a shallow root system may grow well inside, like beets, radishes, a few forms of carrots, lettuces, also with the ideal requirements, even hot tomatoes and peppers. With these kinds of plants, it is more important to set up proper growing methods as outlined in Part One of the book--appropriate airflow, a solid indoor dirt mix, artificial light, insect prevention, and proper containers. Having a designated growing place setup correctly, the fun could start. Although growing mini-crops such as pea shoots is a jaunty project, I find a deep pride in cultivating indoor vegetables, which take the time to create, rewarding me with a plate full of lush salad greens, sweet carrots, peppery radishes, and another bounty in my kitchen garden. Particularly in the spring, even when I am craving new greens, however, just locate West Coast (or globally sent) options in my supermarket, I feel motivated to select a planting frenzy, filling every available area with shelves, lighting, along with just-seeded pots. Perhaps not every vegetable is ideal for my kitchen countertops, however. I have tried many types which may start alright but lack the dirt thickness necessary, or that prosper better outside within the specialty.

Here, we will cover different types of plants which produce the best sense for indoor climbing, and have a peek at specific factors concerning soil, pest avoidance, containers, along with the light. Much like the groundwork for faster-growing plants such as microgreens and pea shoots, effectively developing and harvesting of indoor plants is about the excellent upfront job, paying attention, and preserving that all-important awareness of experience.
Lettuces Before I started farming, then " I had been a salad type of woman. That tag evolved over the years, however: rising, "salad" has been a wedge of iceberg lettuce with ranch dressing and another person (we will sidestep the reality that at Minnesota, "salad" is also Jell-O and Cool Whip), but finally I made my way to a Massive variety of greens,

Such as red oak leaf, butterhead, Bibb, and romaine. I like the mix of textures and colours it's possible to place together with salad combinations, particularly with options such as the 'Freckles' collection that develops with profound splashes of red or 'hazes," which creates tight minds of reddish leaves that conceal a good lime green Centre.

There are many options when it has to do with lettuce variety it just sounds right to kick the plants chapter with this flexible and much- adored vegetable.

Get Prepared Fantastic Varieties for Indoor Growing

At the risk of oversimplifying the array of lettuce options, I will make a general promise: lettuce will come in among two variations --you have head lettuce that is accurate to this definition, or you've got salad combinations that combine lots of varieties and develop in a cluster as opposed to a tightly contained mind. That does not indicate they're two different types--mind lettuces could be contained in a mixture, you merely harvest them if they are still little greens. The gap comes through the seeding process since you space them to adapt for head lettuce expansion in these kinds, or you also seed liberally (although not as significantly as

Microgreens) so which you may harvest several types concurrently. If it comes to indoor climbing, I almost always gravitate into the mixtures because they grow fast, I will seed them based on color dimensions, and they feature a selection of tastes out of mustard greens along with peppery arugula to moderately 'Rouge d'Hiver' and frilly'Lollo Rosso.' Many seed Businesses market their combinations. However, you can also create your own out of contenders like those:

- Arugula: Also called the rocket, this is a reliable alternative for including a peppery taste to sandwiches. The spiky, dark green leaves blend well in a salad but,besides, may be substituted for salmon in individual dishes.
- Green Oakleaf' and 'Red Oakleaf': Maybe Not surprisingly, all these lettuces receive their title for having leaves, which are much like those of pine trees. In cases like this, oak leaf is an umbrella word with various types in that household, for example, as 'Tango," 'Bolsachica,' "Panisse,' and my favorite, 'Sulu' (that I adore because I am a sci-fi nerd). Oakleaf varieties are straightforward to develop and have a tendency to get a mild taste and crunch.
- Baby foliage: Similar to oak leaf, "baby foliage" is a general expression as opposed to a number inside itself. Made to be chosen from a young period of expansion, a few excellent selections for baby leaf lettuce "Red Sails,' "Refugio,' "Parris Island," and 'Defender.' Following is a head's up for seed trimming: a few infant foliage options will also be oak leaf types, but not all

of oak leaf options are designated as infant foliage and confused yet? Do not worry--that the designation does not matter for developing, it is only a means to suggest which lettuces are greatest if harvested in a tiny stage.

- Lollo Rosso': Incredibly frilly and somewhat sour, this lettuce comes with an intense flavor that gets stronger as it becomes more prominent. The reddish leaves have a glowing green splash close to the floor, and it is inclined to be highest when blended with milder lettuces instead of served.

There are numerous types of lettuce, which is an issue of visual and taste preference concerning what you select. I tend to enjoy a little bit of peppery taste, a hint of bitterness, along with a range of greens and reds. If you prefer just mild greens, then elect for one variety that guarantees that color and flavor.

Should you cannot decide and just need several seed types mixed, then select one of those carrot mixes offered from the seed companies which specialize in people. Regardless of what you decide, I would suggest jotting down notes that are growing in a diary. When developing many types of lettuce, then I occasionally forget that which works well and what does not or that which tasted too sour or too dull. A fast perusal of the gardening diary before ordering regularly helps to differentiate the bountiful in the blah.

Trays, Pots, and Additional containers

Because lettuce has a shallow root system, so it also functions nicely within a medium-sized container. I tend to work with hanging baskets since I will move them more efficiently, and since they look beautiful as a focus inside the kitchen, particularly if I am climbing lettuces with loads of crimson leaves. As with other crops, lettuce will perform better in vinyl compared to at terra cotta pots, since the clay will dry out the ground blend quicker compared to plastic. If you enjoy the look of terra cotta, simply pop up a plastic insert into bud. Just be sure that there are holes at the bottom for proper drainage.

Soil Mix

As long as you are not using dirt from the backyard, lettuces can flourish in many different land types. You do not need to play about with drainage options by adding stones or mixing sand into a mulch mix --simply grab a purse of all-purpose potting mixture, and you are all set. The combination ought to be designated and organic for vegetable growth.

Planting and Care First Steps

Fill the pot with dirt, with approximately an inch of distance between the top of the container along with the ground. Sprinkle the carrot seeds in addition to the ground, taking care to divide any which are close to one another. To get a medium-sized bud, you're likely going to use about twenty-five seeds. However, it is not vital to become picky about it and then rely on them out. You do not have to find worried about feeling, possibly, provided that they are not clumped together.

Maintaining Growing

When the lettuces Start to launch, There Are Numerous methods for fostering expansion:

- Water every day to keep the ground moist but not soaked. The Best Way to tell if it needs water is to put your finger around half of an inch into the ground and if it feels dry, water.
- Since lettuces get more prominent, it is generally far better to base water. This usually means filling a bin or sink with a couple of inches of water and then putting the carrot bud into it for approximately ten minutes. Do not Allow the lettuce sit for Quite a While, or accumulate water at a plate below the kettle; this may cause root rot.
- You will observe that many lettuces are sprouting from precisely the same location. Weed from the more reduced energies so the more powerful ones could have more space to expand. When the weeded-out seedlings Appear workable in Any Way, simply transfer them into another pot or consume them because of microgreens.
- Fertilize if expansion looks slow. I do not usually utilize fertilizer to get lettuces because they do not often need the increase, but in case your lettuces are trying to find they might use some Excess nourishment, use a compost once per week for three weeks and see whether this makes a huge difference. Do not use over that, however, or you can "burn" the plant via over-fertilization.

Troubleshooting
It's Been a Week, and There Is No Germination

In case you have been watering gently and providing the lettuces sunlight, then be patient and wait for a second week; occasionally, in certain circumstances, they are sometimes sluggish concerning germination but can prove fine as soon as they begin growing. When it's been a couple of weeks, and there is no germination, then you could be overwatering or placing the bud in a place that is too dim.

The Lettuces Seem Droopy

One of the pleasant things about living in the Midwest is that lettuces do well inside because a lot of this year is trendy (perhaps a bit too much of this year for some people). Lettuce enjoys cooler temperatures and also will flourish most at approximately 60 to 70 degrees Fahrenheit. If you are experiencing higher temperatures or humidity inside your property, consider transferring the lettuce into a more relaxed place.

Harvesting and Preservation Getting prepared to Pick

Harvesting lettuces is a cinch --simply snip them at any given stage of expansion appeals to you. Typically, I favor smaller lettuce greens instead of bigger leaves, so that I cut them if they are just about 6 inches. Regardless of what size you pick, just make sure to prevent the internal leaves of each cluster, because it includes the immature expansion that will cause your next salad.

Storage Factors

Like microgreens, lettuce will maintain the best in containers. Also, they do good in plastic bags put in the crisper drawer of the fridge. Generally, however, it is far better to harvest just what you will need for a specific meal and allow the plant to retain producing lettuce leaves.

TIPS AND TRICKS FOR MICROGEREENS CULTIVATION

Sprouting on a counter, microgreens are an indication of life when you are desperate for a few green. Elegant because garnishes, filled with flavors and zesty notes, also a windowsill harvest of microgreens tastes of spring. And also for the gardener who likes to cook? Mini sprouts move from seed to salad in under 14 days.

1. Locate a bright windowsill.

A southern environment, in which light pops, "provides you stronger crops, with greater taste, color, and longer shelf life" Should you reside in Southern California, as Fitzpatrick does, then expand them outside.

2. Do not overlook drainage.

Pick a menu at least 1.5 inches deep, with empty holes.

3. Utilize a seed starting mixture.

A fluffy, lightweight dirt, such as EB Stone's Seed Starter Mix, can help tiny sprouts develop. Fill out a plate with 1 inch of seed starting mixture and completely wet the dirt so it is moist (not dripping) in the outside to the ground.

4. Think past lettuce.

"I love sunflower microgreens, however there is plenty of interesting things on the market, such as radish, dull bok, bok choi, red amaranth, arugula, lettuce, and mustard greens," says Fitzpatrick.

5. Scatter seeds around one-eighth into a quarter inch apart.

"It is not a specific science, and therefore don't be worried if you end up over-seeding. I discover more is far better than," says Fitzpatrick. Cover the seeds evenly using a different half-inch coating of seedling mixture and moist down that too.

6. Jump fertilizer.

Microgreens are in reality cotyledon leaves, meaning they are the first ones to moan following germination. They want only water and sun to develop. Based upon the seeds, then you may notice sprouting shoots at three to five times.

7. Mist, and do not overwater.

Heavy watering can crush seedlings or lead to mould to grow in the dirt.

8. Harvest.

Many microgreens will be prepared for harvest in 10 to 14 days. Cut them in clusters only above the soil line. Drink cold water and consume.

9. Repeat.

Once you crop, microgreens don't grow back again. For a constant supply, it is possible to reuse the soil by turning it on. Sprinkle seeds, and then cover with another layer of dirt. The origins in the former crop will have produced a mat which will gradually mulch itself," says Fitzpatrick, "therefore it is all very self-sustaining."

Conclusion

I strongly suggest that you simply choose gardening designs and techniques which will agree with your lifestyle, and just consider aquaponics gardening if you are really committed to your own plants and animals, and would be happy to put effort and time into it.

I hope that one day in the near future you'll find yourself one of your plants and fishes and will think of this book, and will probably be grateful that instead of visiting the supermarket you have the absolute liberty of picking your own dinner from plants that you have lovingly tended.

For a closing note, I want to thank you for taking the time to read this publication. Through the duration of this publication, we have demonstrated you the ins and outs of the chances of aquaponics systems. Please choose a lesson from the book and apply them to the actual world.

In gardening, and particularly in indoor gardening using its catchy nuances, it can be simple to feel defeated occasionally. Despite all of my cheerleading throughout this publication, I have experienced lots of frustration once I see mold, aphids, or even crumpled leaves. The toughest moments are the ones when I glance at a pot of dirt mix and understand that there is supposed to be quite a small sweet sprout poking through vermiculite, and I have nothing.

However, I comfort myself with the recognition that this is a work-in-progress, which adaptability and versatility are characteristics to notify not just my gardening, but also my perspective on virtually everything. While I believe that way, I visit my small indoor garden for a sign of everything I would like to nurture in my entire life: nutrition, attention, awareness, and happiness. Revel in that burst of gratification that accompanies watching a plant start to sprout from the ground, and love that sense as it conveys all of the ways into the minute that you serve it within a meal. In lots of ways, us, it not only produces a link between our meals but also on our communities and our world.

CPSIA information can be obtained
at www.ICGtesting.com
Printed in the USA
BVHW011407030521
606322BV00004B/418

 9 781667 137544